ANCIENT EARTH JOURNAL

THE EARLY CRETACEOUS

NOTES, DRAWINGS, AND OBSERVATIONS FROM PREHISTORY

BY JUAN CARLOS ALONSO & GREGORY S. PAUL

*For Dalí, may you never lose
your sense of wonder.
Love, Dad.*

© 2015 Quarto Publishing Group USA Inc.
Published by Walter Foster Jr., an imprint of Quarto Publishing Group USA Inc.
All rights reserved. Walter Foster Jr. is trademarked.
Artwork © Juan Carlos Alonso
Written by Juan Carlos Alonso and Gregory S. Paul
Illustrated by Juan Carlos Alonso

Publisher: Anne Landa
Creative Director: Shelley Baugh
Production Director: Yuhong Guo
Editorial Director: Pauline Molinari
Senior Editor: Stephanie Meissner
Managing Editor: Karen Julian
Associate Editor: Jennifer Gaudet
Developmental Editor: Janessa Osle
Editorial Assistant: Julie Chapa
Production Designer: Debbie Aiken

www.walterfoster.com
6 Orchard Road, Suite 100
Lake Forest, CA 92630

Printed in China, May 2015
1 3 5 7 9 10 8 6 4 2
1767

Table of Contents

Forewords

Philip J. Currie, MSc, PhD, FRSC
Professor and Canada Research Chair, Dinosaur Paleobiology
University of Alberta, Edmonton, Canada

Once a dark period in the geological history of the Earth, the Early Cretaceous is rapidly becoming one of the best-understood periods of the Mesozoic Era (often called the Age of Reptiles). The Early Cretaceous is bracketed between the spectacular Late Jurassic and Late Cretaceous periods; fossil-bearing sites suggest huge changes took place in the faunas and floras during this time. In short, major transformations took place in the Early Cretaceous that signaled the beginning of the modern world. Over the last two decades, incredible fossils from this time period have been found all over the world.

Driven by the origin and rise of flowering plants, environments were starting to become more "modern" in appearance, promoting the evolution of insects, lizards, snakes, dinosaurs, birds, and mammals at unprecedented rates. However, it would still be more than 50 million years before non-avian dinosaurs would die out, along with flying reptiles and so many other animals.

As a palaeontologist who works mostly with Late Cretaceous dinosaurs, I would love to climb into a time machine and be transported back a hundred million years or so. Sitting in an Early Cretaceous forest with my pencil and notebook, camera, and sketchbook, I would try to understand the big changes that were imminent—dinosaurs were about to go into their last great flowering, with very different things happening in the northern and southern hemispheres. I would keep my eyes open for the dangerous dinosaurs, of course, especially predators such as the dog-sized Deinonychus and the giant Acrocanthosaurus. (That might be hard to do, however, because it would be so fascinating to watch the little feathered theropods like the Microraptor hunting lizards, mammals, and birds, while flocks of essentially modern birds mixed with more primitive toothed or long-tailed relatives!)

Although it will never be possible for me to travel physically back to that wonderful time, *The Early Cretaceous* has the feel of a naturalist's notebook to conjure up such illusions and dreams. I hope these wonderful images have the same effect on you!

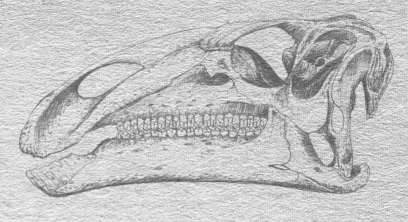

Matthew T. Mossbrucker

Director & Chief Curator

Morrison Natural History Museum, Morrison, Colorado

So that's what they think dinosaurs looked like? I have seen this scenario play out in museum exhibits on scores of occasions. Curious visitors introduced to life history via art. This synergy between paleontologists, who are charged with the study of fossil life forms, and specially trained artists is vital for intuitively communicating past life on earth.

Those of us who are charged with interpreting fossils for the masses have come to rely on this special type of artist, the "paleoartist," to help us resurrect animals and plants from the deep recesses of time. Paleoartists are the unsung heroes of science literacy. Their vital skills translate the inanimate remains of long-dead creatures once again into living beasts. They inspire a connection between our world and the countless ecosystems that have come and gone before us.

Perhaps nothing stirs the imagination like dinosaurs—monstrous and exotic forms brought to life through the imagination of artistic scientists like Juan Carlos Alonso and Gregory S. Paul. This book is a wonderful blend of imagination and reality and a testament to the powerful partnership between art and science.

Cycad plants and leaf detail

Introduction

Imagine stepping back in time 120 million years to the Early Cretaceous period and walking around on an earth similar to today's, yet in many regards, almost alien.

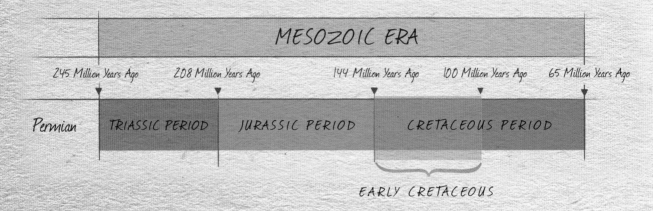

The Early Cretaceous is the last period of the Mesozoic Era, or "the age of the reptiles." The earth is undergoing monumental changes; the once giant supercontinent is slowly drifting apart. The tectonic plates are tearing apart along a great fiery rift, forming the early North Atlantic Ocean. South America and Africa are still partly attached to one another, while close by Antarctica, Australia, and India are bundled into one continent.

A massive shallow sea covers large areas, turning Europe into an archipelago of islands similar to today's Indonesia. The great tropical Tethys Ocean divides Asia from the southern continents and the vast Pacific Ocean is the largest it will ever be.

As you travel through the Early Cretaceous, you will experience warm temperatures throughout most of the world. Seasons consist of a dry and a wet period. Approaching the poles, winters are dark and very cold.

You will see glaciers gracing some highlands, especially in the southernmost areas. As you cross the center of the continents, you will encounter endless arid deserts, making your journey difficult, if not impossible. Areas of abundant plant life are widespread, with the ground covered in waist-high ferns forming broad prairies in drier flatlands.

As you travel through forests, you will see short cycads, gingko trees, and enormous canopies of towering conifers. Small flowering shrubs—the first to appear on the earth—decorate the banks of streams and creeks. You can't walk through fields of grass nor can you see hardwood trees, including oak or walnut, as they haven't evolved yet. A lot of the animal life will look familiar to you. Small bodies of water are home to frogs, turtles, and salamanders.

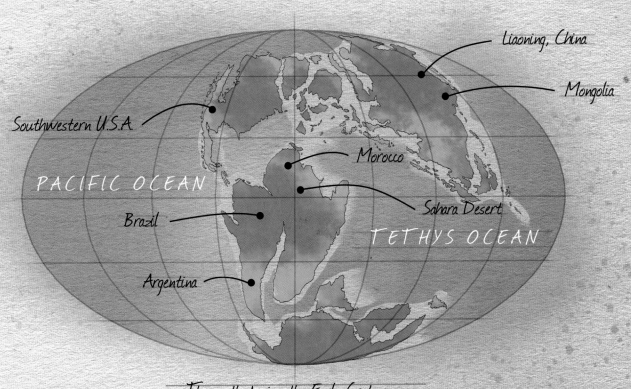

The earth during the Early Cretaceous

You might find lizards and rodent-sized mammals scurrying through the underbrush as well as burrowing into the ground. The insects look familiar too; you will spot dragonflies, flies, fleas, roaches, social termites, wasps, and moths. In many ways, the Early Cretaceous will remind you of several places on earth today. But in other ways, it is an incredibly different world.

Much of the wildlife of the Early Cretaceous period is simply extraordinary! Animals have adapted for survival in a dinosaur-dominated environment so savage that it's unsafe for people to move about unless they are armed.

Deadly two-legged, long-tailed predators the length of a city bus and swifter than any human roam freely, each capable of swallowing a man whole. (It's no wonder that some herbivorous dinosaurs are armored like tanks!) Others are land whales weighing up to 100 tons and measuring five stories tall! These creatures move in huge herds, wrecking the umbrella-shaped conifers they feed upon. Yet other big herbivorous dinosaurs look like crosses between massive cattle and ducks, with flat beaks designed for tearing into plants.

Pinecones

Conifer branch and needles

Not all of the Early Cretaceous dinosaurs are big, however. In fact, most are fairly small and often feathered like birds. Most of the small dinosaurs are beaked plant-eaters and fast on their two legs. Many are

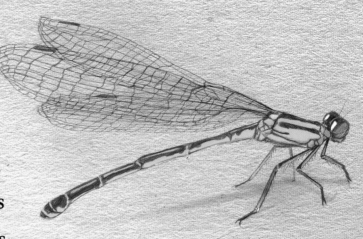

bipedal predators. Some have sickle-shaped razor claws on their inner toes used to disembowel their prey. The dinosaurs most closely related to birds have wings on both of their arms and legs that they use to fly between trees and pounce on prey from above. Birds as we now know them today are just beginning to appear. They often live in enormous flocks, giving some stiff competition to the flying pterosaurs that had long ruled the skies. Pterosaurs are growing larger, sporting enormous head crests and shorter tails.

Now imagine living alongside these animals, recording and sketching every possible detail of their lives in your journal. The premise of this book is to bring these magnificent animals to life for you through art and science. Discover the Early Cretaceous world and its life through new eyes, and get to know the personalities of each species. Discover how sauropods with heads five stories above the ground could pump blood to their brains under extreme pressures. Discover how dinosaurs learned to fly as they developed wings. See how some dinosaurs survived polar blizzards, while others lived through desert heat. This journal gives you a visual guide to what it must have been like to experience possibly the strangest wildlife the earth has ever seen and may never see again.

Welcome to the Early Cretaceous.

The Theropods

Few animals, living or extinct, inspire as much awe and terror as the theropod dinosaurs. Think what it would be like to be in the Early Cretaceous and encounter an animal 40 feet long with a head the size of your body and sharp teeth 8 inches long. Its small eyes are fixed on you as it catches your scent. You try to run, but it's much faster than you. You try to hide, but its highly developed olfactory senses can smell you no matter where you are. You are no match for the greatest predator to ever exist. Luckily, an encounter such as this will never happen, but the descendants of the great theropod dinosaurs live among us in the form of birds.

6 feet

3 feet

Theropods, meaning "beast-footed," are a diverse group of dinosaurs that lived throughout the Mesozoic Era. They are classified as saurischian dinosaurs, or "lizard-hipped" (because of the structure of their hips), and are mostly recognized for being bipedal. Theropod species ranged in size from miniscule, 12 inches in length, to the super predators measuring over 50 feet long.

With a few exceptions, theropod bodies were slender with longer hind limbs, shorter forelimbs, and a long tail. Their hands usually had three fingers and were used for specialized functions such as

flight or grasping prey; in some cases, they were atrophied to the point of near uselessness. Their feet contained four toes, three of which made contact with the ground and were used for walking and running. Theropod skeletons were constructed of thin-walled, hollow bones with relatively large skulls. Most theropod skulls have several holes in their structure; these holes are called "fenestra," and their purpose was to make the heads lighter, sometimes allowing for larger and heavier teeth.

Most theropods were carnivorous, feeding on other dinosaurs, insects, and fish; others were herbivorous, feeding only on plants. Some were omnivorous, feeding both on plants and meat. While all are fascinating, it is the carnivorous theropods that inspire the most awe. With an arsenal of

Egg tooth

Theropod hatchling

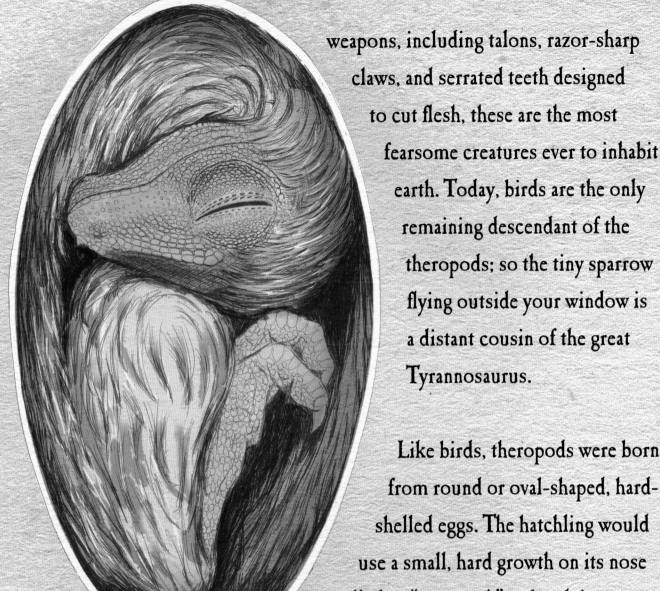

Theropod inside egg

weapons, including talons, razor-sharp claws, and serrated teeth designed to cut flesh, these are the most fearsome creatures ever to inhabit earth. Today, birds are the only remaining descendant of the theropods; so the tiny sparrow flying outside your window is a distant cousin of the great Tyrannosaurus.

Like birds, theropods were born from round or oval-shaped, hard-shelled eggs. The hatchling would use a small, hard growth on its nose called an "egg tooth" to break its way out of the shell. This egg tooth would fall off its nose soon after emerging from the egg. And, also like birds, several species are known to have cared for their young by feeding and protecting them.

Theropods were also diverse in their skin textures and coverings. Some bodies were covered in a fine filament, called "protofeathers," some in a mosaic of smooth and bumpy scales, and others were covered in feathers and even had fully functioning wings.

The Theropods of the Early Cretaceous

Following the Jurassic Period, apex predators like Allosaurus and Torvosaurus were replaced by Acrocanthosaurus atokensis and Carcharodontosaurus saharicus. Bigger, stronger species evolved to fill their role at the top of the food chain. While some predators became larger, new species like Utahraptor ostrommaysorum, with its sickle-shaped killing claw, also found their place in the Early Cretaceous. Flying raptor dinosaurs continued to evolve with species like Microraptor gui, which used wings on both its legs and arms to glide through trees and capture prey.

In some cases, it was the adaptation to specific prey that made the theropods unique. Baryonyx walkeri developed strong muscular arms with hooked claws and a long snout with conical teeth all designed to grasp fish. Not all adaptations were about hunting; Concavenator corcovatus evolved strange hump structures on its back used as a display to attract mates. This was an amazing period in earth's history. In the following pages you will experience these animals in detail, species by species, and witness the theropods of the Early Cretaceous.

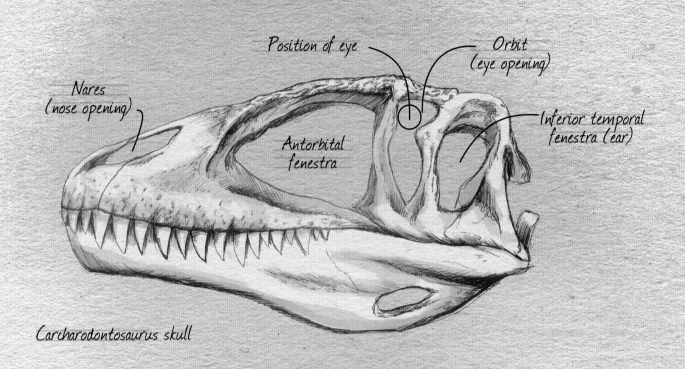

Nares
(nose opening)

Position of eye

Orbit
(eye opening)

Antorbital
fenestra

Inferior temporal
fenestra (ear)

Carcharodontosaurus skull

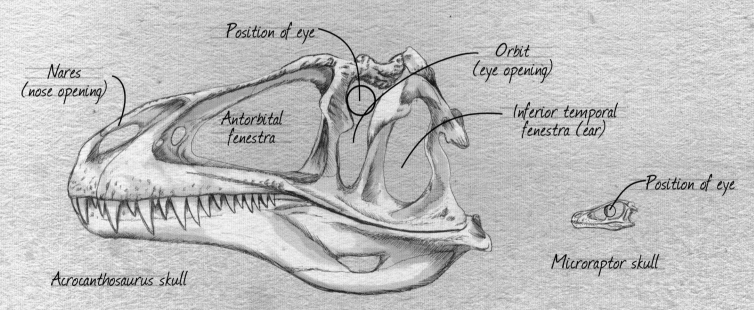

Position of eye

Nares
(nose opening)

Orbit
(eye opening)

Antorbital
fenestra

Inferior temporal
fenestra (ear)

Position of eye

Acrocanthosaurus skull

Microraptor skull

Acrocanthosaurus atokensis

Location Observed: Oklahoma, Texas, and Wyoming, United States

Family: Carcharodontosauridae

Length: 35 feet (11 meters)

Height: 14 feet (4.5 meters)

Weight: 4.4 tons

Temperament: Solitary, very aggressive

Dermal growth on head

Elongated dorsal spines form a sail along back and top of tail

Powerfully built small hands and arms

Muscular legs

Two irregular crests
along top of head

Small eyes

Large serrated teeth
partially covered by lip

Large jaw muscles

6 feet

3 feet

Acrocanthosaurus is the apex predator of its area

17

Large sail across back

Coarse scales in
rows across back

18

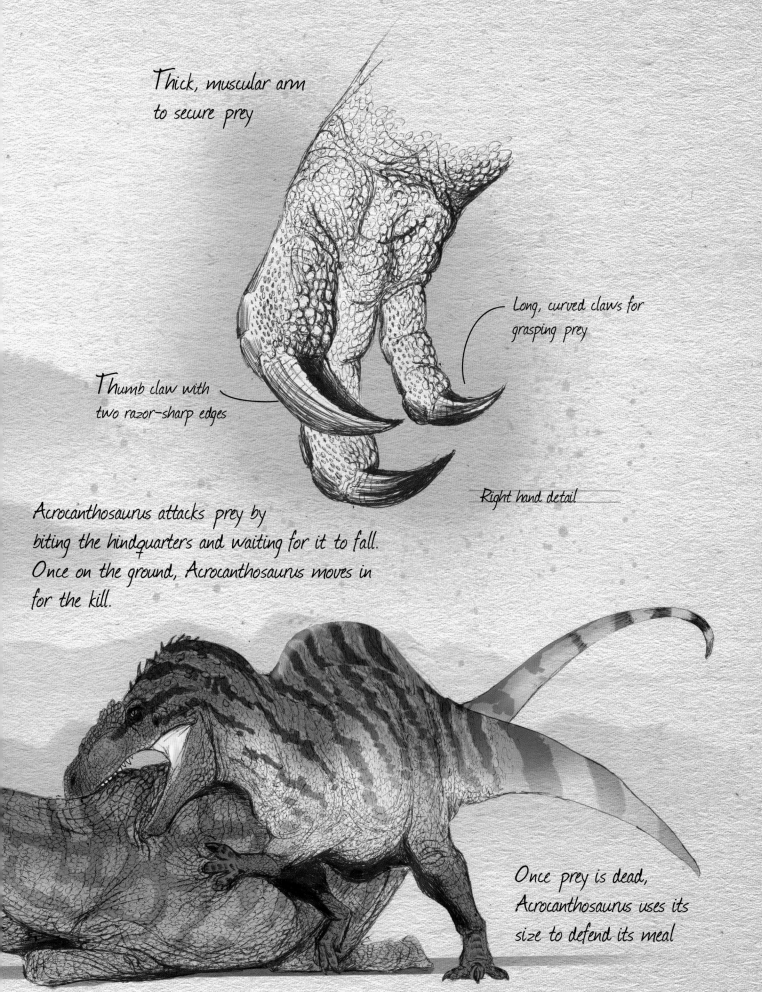

Thick, muscular arm
to secure prey

Long, curved claws for
grasping prey

Thumb claw with
two razor-sharp edges

Right hand detail

Acrocanthosaurus attacks prey by
biting the hindquarters and waiting for it to fall.
Once on the ground, Acrocanthosaurus moves in
for the kill.

Once prey is dead,
Acrocanthosaurus uses its
size to defend its meal

Baryonyx walkeri

Location Observed: *Southeast England, Weald Clay*

Family: *Spinosauridae*

Length: *25 feet (7.5 meters)*

Height: *12 feet (3.8 meters)*

Weight: *1.2 tons*

Temperament: *Solitary, territorial, aggressive*

Long neck

Well-developed shoulders

Massive claws
on forelimbs

Powerful arms

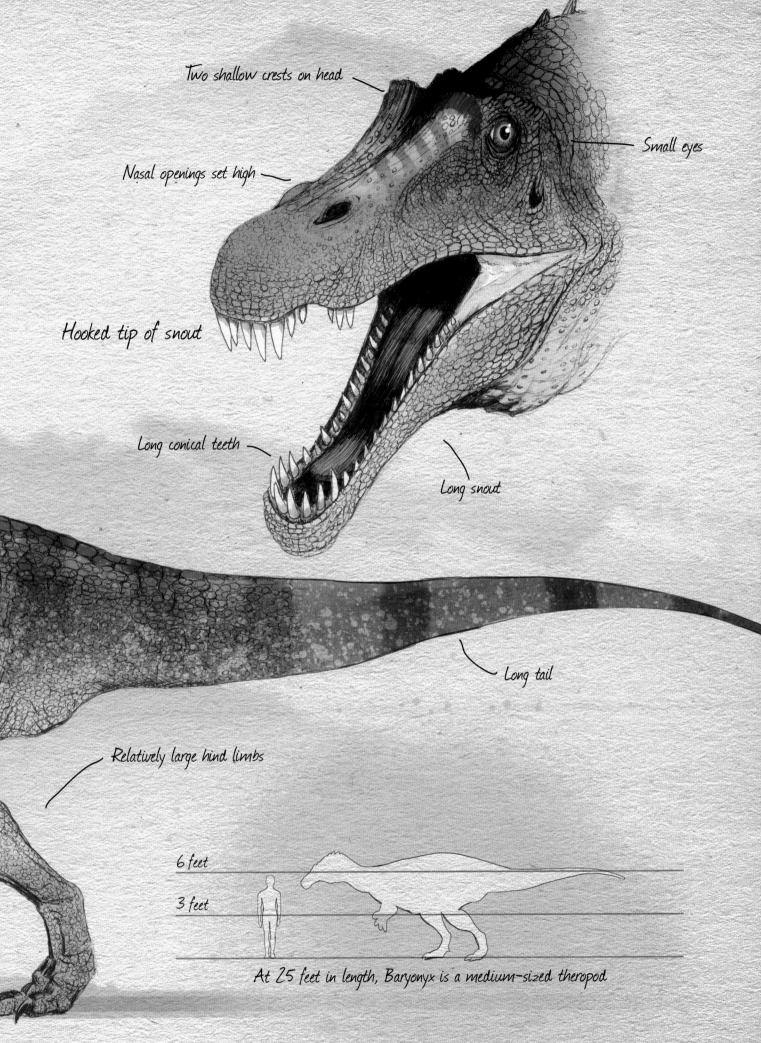

Two shallow crests on head

Small eyes

Nasal openings set high

Hooked tip of snout

Long conical teeth

Long snout

Long tail

Relatively large hind limbs

6 feet

3 feet

At 25 feet in length, Baryonyx is a medium-sized theropod

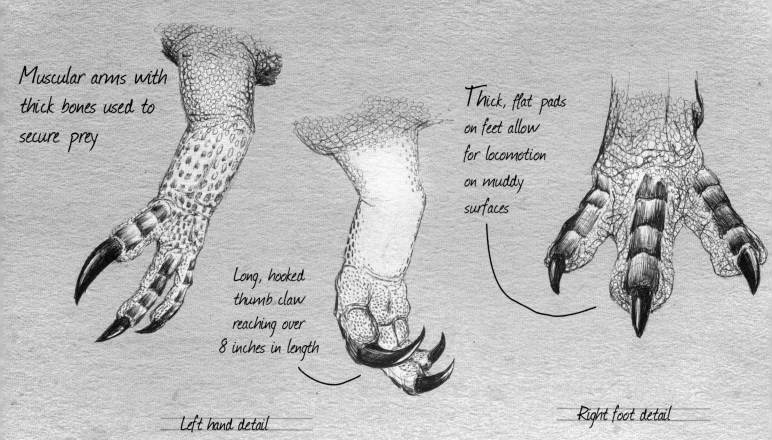

Muscular arms with thick bones used to secure prey

Thick, flat pads on feet allow for locomotion on muddy surfaces

Long, hooked thumb claw reaching over 8 inches in length

Left hand detail

Right foot detail

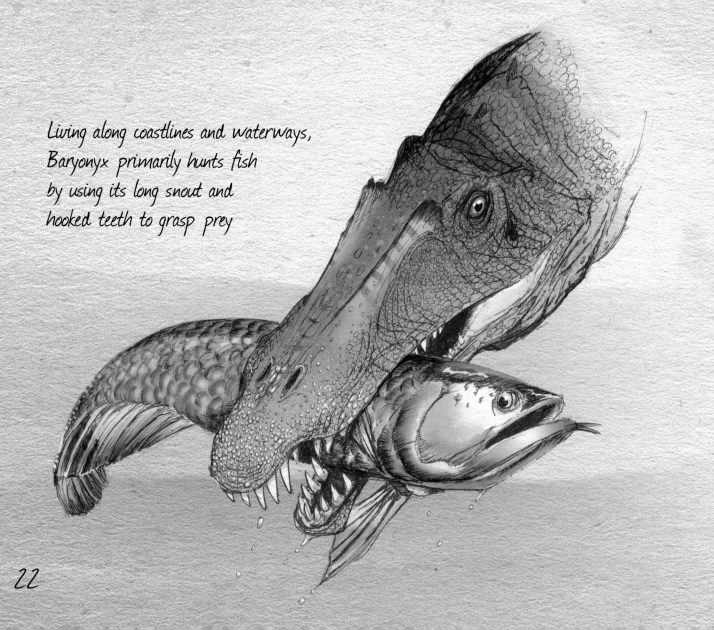

Living along coastlines and waterways, Baryonyx primarily hunts fish by using its long snout and hooked teeth to grasp prey

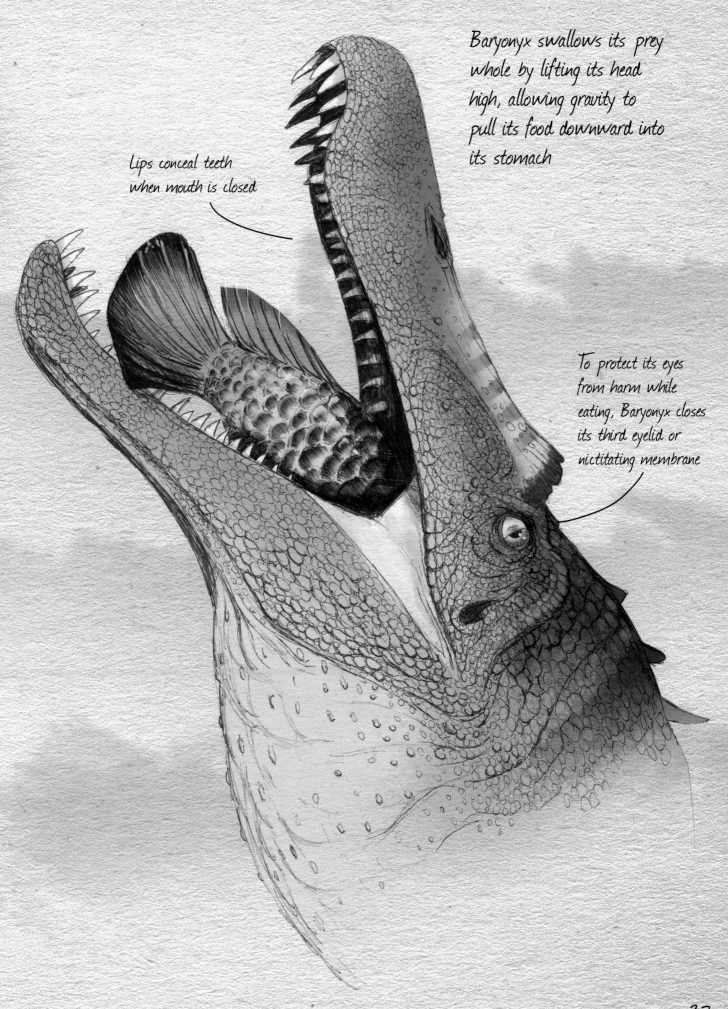

Lips conceal teeth
when mouth is closed

Baryonyx swallows its prey
whole by lifting its head
high, allowing gravity to
pull its food downward into
its stomach

To protect its eyes
from harm while
eating, Baryonyx closes
its third eyelid or
nictitating membrane

23

Beipiaosaurus inexpectus

Location Observed: Liaoning, China

Family: Therizinosauroidae

Length: 6 feet (2.2 meters)

Height: 3 feet (1 meter)

Weight: 90 lbs. (40 kg)

Temperament: Cautious, shy

Hard tip used for digging

Long beak

Feathered crest on head

Small teeth

Curved jaw

Tail covered in feathers

6 feet

3 feet

Beipiaosaurus is about the size of a cassowary

Long, brightly colored,
iridescent feathers on back

Large eyes

Three-toed feet

Right hand detail

Long fingers are
concealed under
plumage

Long, curved claws used primarily
for digging for food

Wing feathers

Claws are retracted
underneath wing

Threat display

Pulls head up
with mouth open

Spreads wings and
claws outward to
appear larger

Stiff tail acts as a
counterbalance

Beipiaosaurus eats primarily grubs
and small burrowing animals. It
hunts using its claws to dig into
decayed wood or soil and then
plunging its hard beak into the hole
to pull out its prey.

Carcharodontosaurus saharicus

Location Observed: *Morocco, Africa*

Family: *Carcharodontosauridae*

Length: *40 feet (12 meters)*

Height: *13 feet (4 meters)*

Weight: *6 tons*

Temperament: *Extremely aggressive, solitary*

Small crest of dermal growth on head

Powerful arms and claws

Massive hind limbs

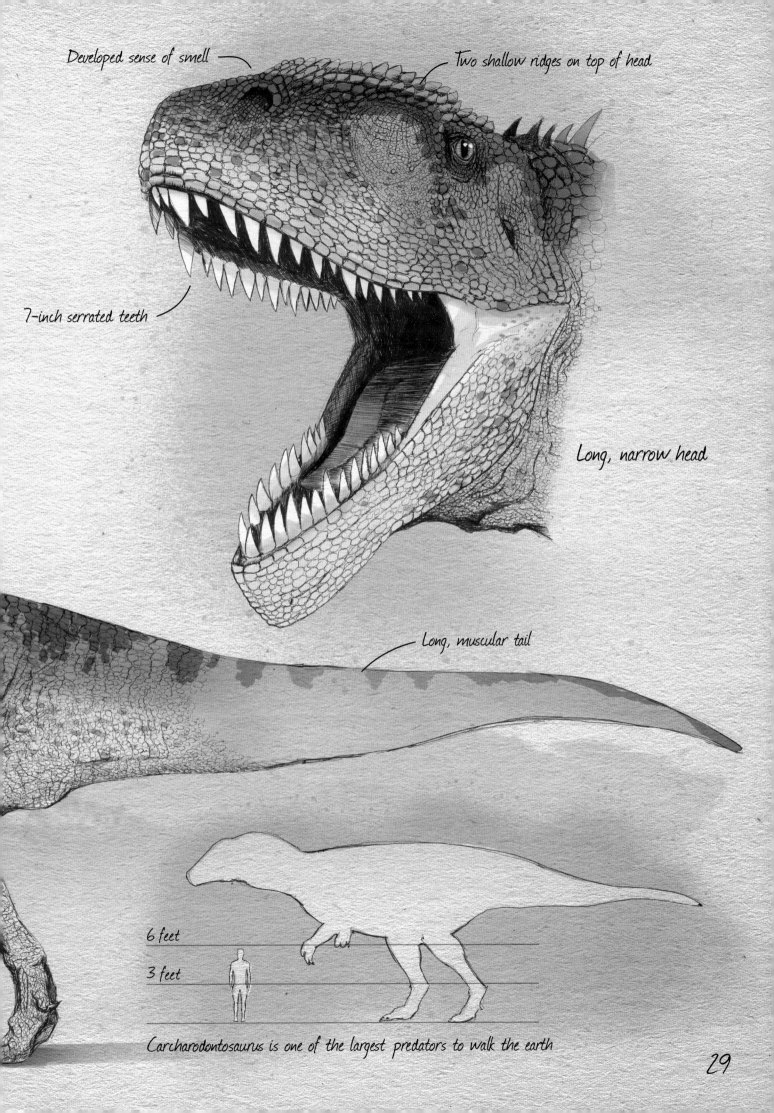

Developed sense of smell

Two shallow ridges on top of head

7-inch serrated teeth

Long, narrow head

Long, muscular tail

6 feet

3 feet

Carcharodontosaurus is one of the largest predators to walk the earth

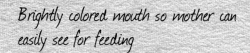
Brightly colored mouth so mother can easily see for feeding

Born covered in downy feathers for insulation

Egg tooth used to break through egg shell

Carcharodontosaurus hatchling

Two weeks old

Feathers and hair are replaced with scales

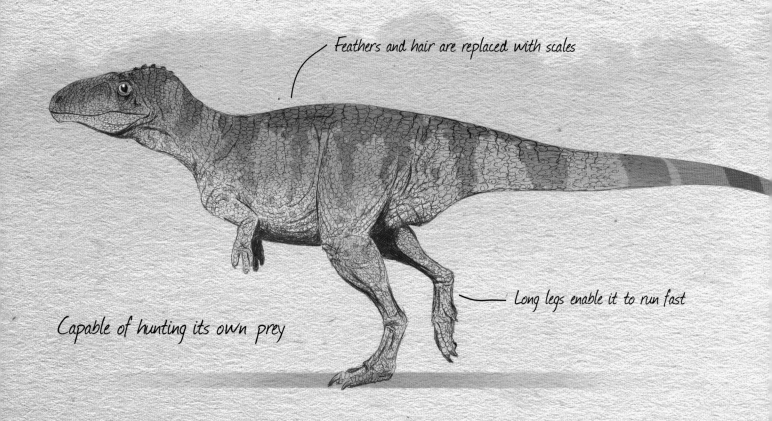

Long legs enable it to run fast

Capable of hunting its own prey

One year old
Approximately 6 feet long

The apex predator of its time, an adult Carcharodontosaurus has no rivals

An adult is strong enough to overpower prey twice its size or take over another predator's kill

31

Concavenator corcovatus

Location Observed: Cuenca, Spain

Family: Carcharodontosauridae

Length: 25 feet (7.5 meters)

Height: 14 feet (4.5 meters)

Weight: 1.2 tons

Temperament: Territorial, aggressive

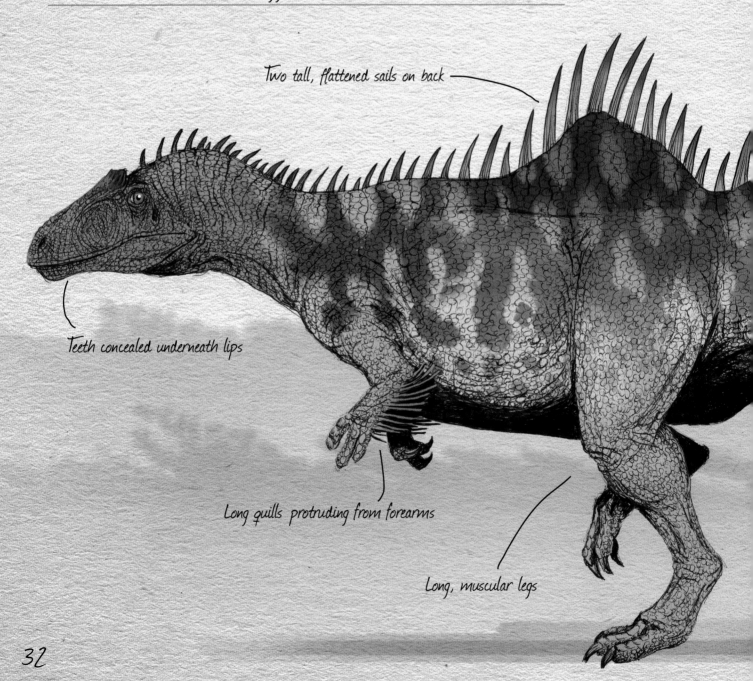

Two tall, flattened sails on back

Teeth concealed underneath lips

Long quills protruding from forearms

Long, muscular legs

Two crests over eyes

Low crest above
nasal openings

Large, serrated teeth

Narrow jaw

Large jaw muscle

Long dermal spines along back

6 feet

3 feet

At 25 feet in length, Concavenator is a medium-sized theropod

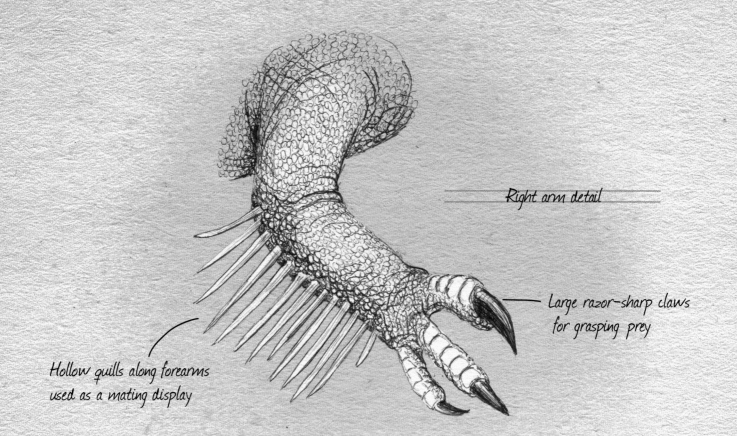

Right arm detail

Large razor-sharp claws
for grasping prey

Hollow quills along forearms
used as a mating display

Using a burst of speed,
Concavenator secures its prey

Pelecanimimus polyodon

When facing its prey, Concavenator
presents a narrow profile

Microraptor gui

Location Observed: Liaoning, China

Family: Dromaeosauridae

Length: 2.5 feet (.7 meter)

Height: 2.6 feet (.75 meter) wingspan

Weight: 1.3 lbs (.6 kg)

Temperament: Reclusive, cautious

Large eyes to hunt at night
and in low-light conditions

Small teeth

Microraptor emits a high-pitched
squawk to warn others to stay
clear of its territory

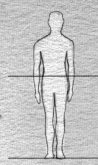

3 feet

Microraptor is about the size of a hawk

Three claws on its hands

Large sickle-like claws on its feet

Microraptor glides for great distances, allowing it to ambush prey without giving away its position

Wings on its legs

Tail detail

Bright colors on tail act as a
display to attract mates

Iridescent blue-black feathers cover body

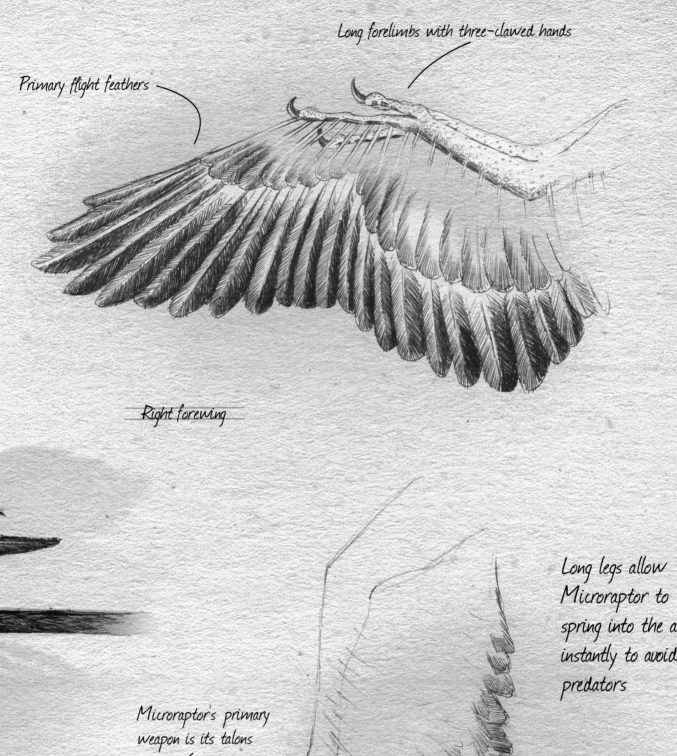

Primary flight feathers

Long forelimbs with three-clawed hands

Right forewing

Long legs allow Microraptor to spring into the air instantly to avoid predators

Microraptor's primary weapon is its talons

Left hind wing

Scipionyx samniticus

Location Observed: Central Italy

Family: Compsognathidae

Length: 5 feet (1.5 meters)

Height: 1.5 feet (.5 meters)

Weight: 6 lbs (2.6 Kg)

Temperament: Shy, elusive

Long, slender body

Long neck

Three-fingered hands with sharp claws

Long legs designed to run fast

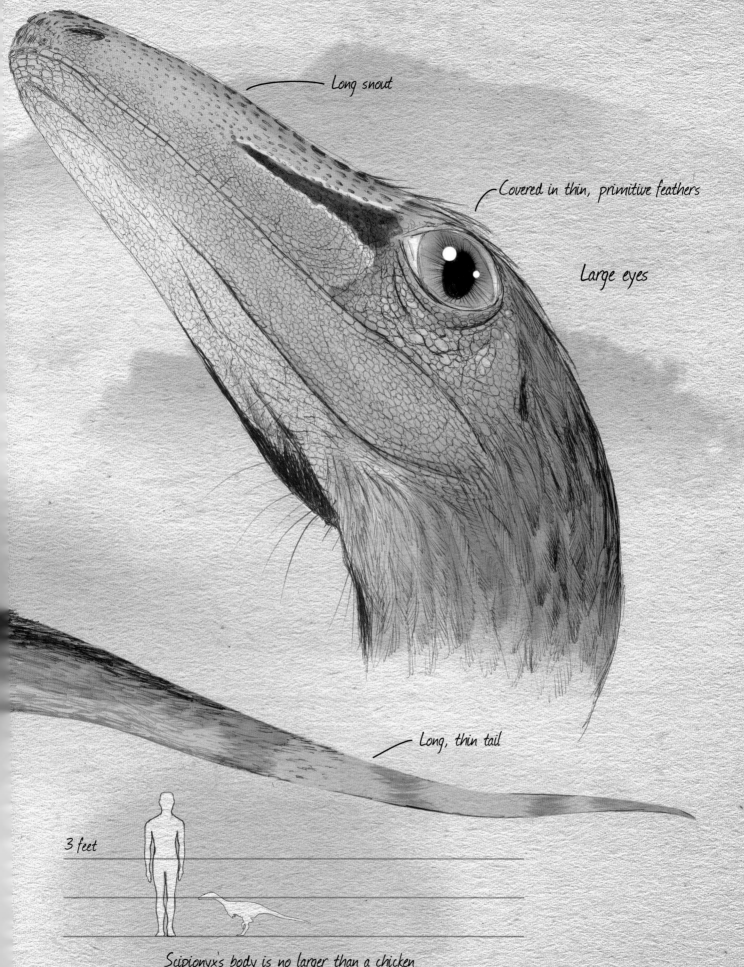

Long snout

Covered in thin, primitive feathers

Large eyes

Long, thin tail

3 feet

Scipionyx's body is no larger than a chicken

41

Covered in downy feathers

Very large eyes

External
ear opening

Large, exposed teeth

Juvenile Scipionyx
Approximately one week old

Like modern birds,
Scipionyx cares for
its young until
they are old enough
to fend for themselves

Their diet consists
of fish, insects, and
even small reptiles

Scipionyx chicks
Three days old

Utahraptor ostrommaysorum

Location Observed: Utah, United States

Family: Dromaeosauridae

Length: 18 feet (5.5 meters)

Height: 7 feet (2.1 meters)

Weight: 600 lbs (272 Kg)

Temperament: Extremely aggressive

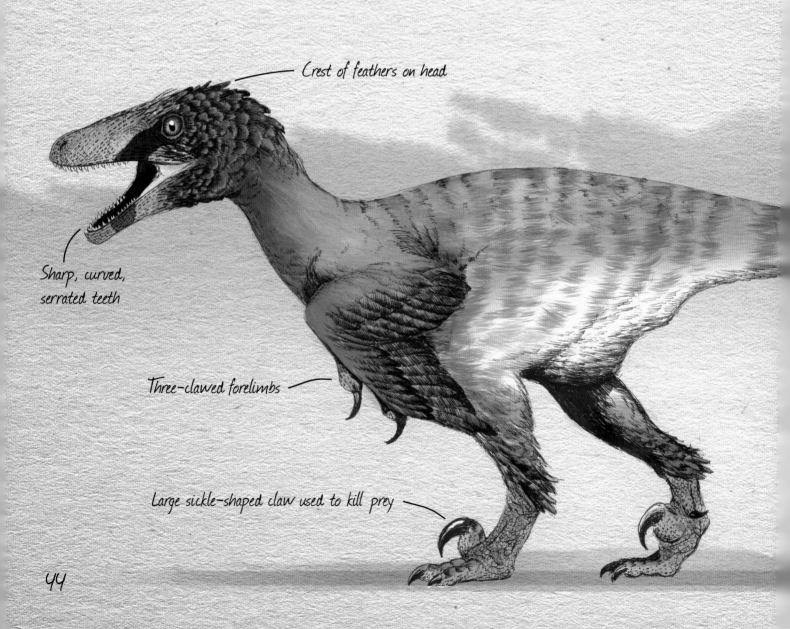

Crest of feathers on head

Sharp, curved, serrated teeth

Three-clawed forelimbs

Large sickle-shaped claw used to kill prey

Large, forward-facing eyes

Feathers cover entire body

Lips conceal teeth

Long, stiff tail

Feather display at end of tail

6 feet

3 feet

Utahraptor is the largest known raptor

45

Beneath the wing plumage
lies a deadly weapon

Three-clawed hands
designed for gripping and
holding prey

Utahraptor right wing detail

A Utahraptor pack
hunting an Iguanadon

Utahraptor hunts in packs

By isolating one animal from the heard, Utahraptor uses its speed and weapons to bring down prey much heavier than itself

Utahraptor's stiff tail acts as a counterbalance to shift its weight from one side to the other

Utahraptor's large killing claw is always kept in an upright position to prevent wear

Utahraptor left foot detail

Its short wings are used to keep its balance

47

Yutyrannus huali

Location Observed: Liaoning, China

Family: Tyrannosauroidea

Length: 30 feet (9 meters)

Height: 9.5 feet (3 meters)

Weight: 2.5 tons

Temperament: Aggressive, territorial, very social

Feather-like fur covering its entire body, including the tail

Muscular arms with large claws for grabbing prey

Powerful legs

Bony crest along the top of its head

Two horns

Large, serrated teeth

Long, slender tail

6 feet

3 feet

Yutyrannus measures 30 feet from head to tail

Yutyrannus hunts in packs
(which sometimes includes its young)

Once prey is caught, it is moved
to a safe place to eat

Yutyrannus left foot detail

To protect themselves from the cold weather, Yutyrannus huddle together to preserve their body temperature

Adult Yutyrannus

Juvenile (7 years old)

Yutyrannus left hand detail

51

The Sauropods

As you walk through the Early Cretaceous landscape, you find yourself near a clearing in the trees. Just ahead of you is a dry lake bed. You look up and notice you are ankle-high with an animal as tall as a building and as wide as a whale! The earth trembles as the creature drops its massive foot to the ground. Around you there are hundreds of these animals walking together in a great herd across the landscape looking for food. Their massive necks are slowly swaying forward with each step. You feel the constant rumble under your feet and hear sporadic trumpeting as if announcing their arrival. You are in the presence of true giants, the largest animals to ever walk the earth—the sauropods.

6 feet

3 feet

Sauropods were an extraordinary group of dinosaurs belonging to the saurischian family, named for the lizard-like structure of their hips. The name sauropod, meaning "lizard-footed" in Greek, was given to these animals in 1878 by paleontologist O.C. Marsh upon discovering their huge legs and feet. Their long necks and whip-like tails made them easy to recognize. All of them stood on four legs, some reaching lengths of over 100 feet (30 meters) and weighing more than 50 tons. (That's longer than any animal that has ever lived, including the blue whale!) The very first sauropod species appeared in the late Triassic Period.

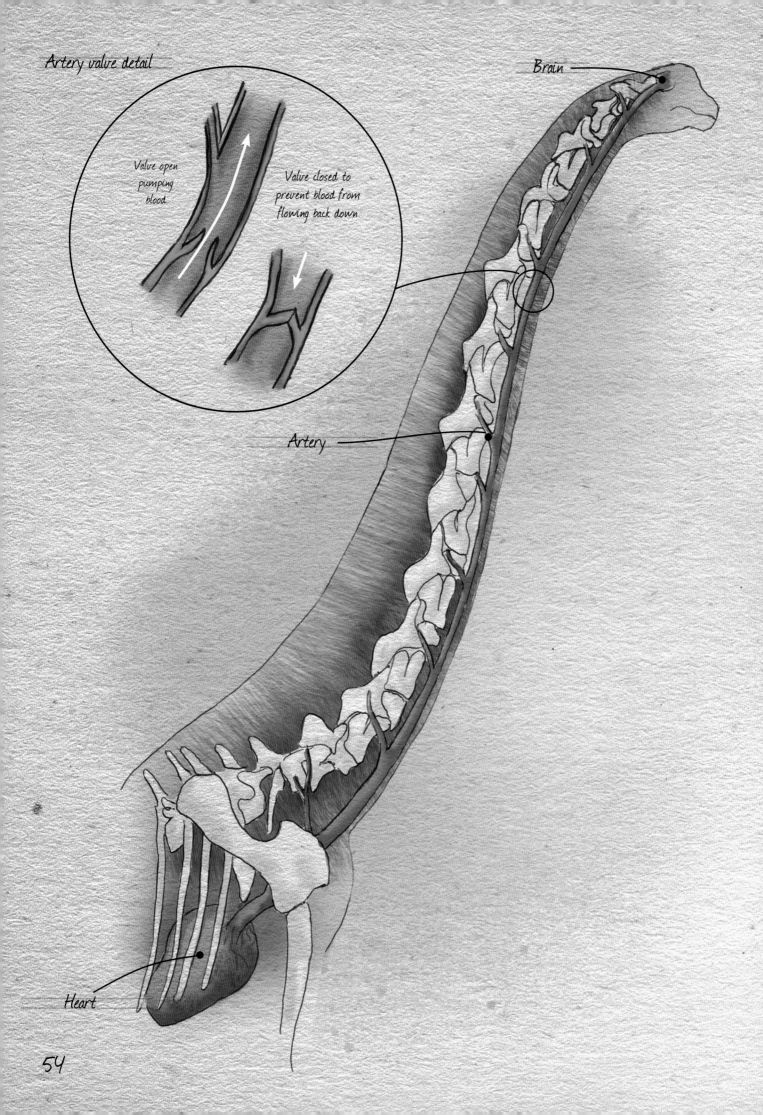

Artery valve detail

Valve open
pumping
blood

Valve closed to
prevent blood from
flowing back down

Brain

Artery

Heart

Its descendants thrived until the end of the age of dinosaurs, about 150 million years—by far the most successful herbivorous group of land animals in history. By the late Jurassic Period, sauropods filled the landscape with great thunderous herds of Brachiosaurs, Diplodocus, and other enormous species stretching as far as the eye could see. They dominated the land; this was the time of giants. The sauropods continued to evolve into diverse species through the Early Cretaceous, giving us some of the largest and most fascinating animals that ever existed.

Sauropods' bodies were rather short in comparison to their necks and tails. Their legs were thick, sturdy, and strong, similar to an elephant's. They supported the weight of their massive necks and tails through tall spines in their backbones, which acted much like a suspension bridge, allowing both the neck and tail to swing independently while anchored to the body. Some had tails as long as their necks and bodies combined. They would use their tails as immense whips swaying constantly, protecting their hindquarters from attack. Some had upright necks that extended 70 feet into the air, as tall as a 7-story building. In order to pump blood to their heads, sauropods developed massive hearts and a network of blood vessels complete with valves that prevented blood from flowing back down due to the force of gravity. This enabled them to maintain blood pressure whether eating from the treetops or drinking from the ground.

For their enormous body size and weight, sauropods had tiny brains. A brain no larger than a tennis ball controlled their immense body, so they moved with a slow gait from tree to tree in order to find food. However, not all sauropods were whale-sized; some were only 30 to 40 feet in length, filling evolutionary niches by not getting too large to compete with the giants.

Sauropods' skulls were lightly built with the nasal opening set far back, closer to the eyes. Sauropods generally had small teeth lining the front edge of the skull, which they used to strip leaves from the branches of trees or cut leaves and stems from cycads or ferns. Most of the taller species fed on pine needles and cones from towering conifer trees. None had developed larger teeth for chewing, so all the plant matter was directly swallowed and deposited into their immense stomachs. Most would swallow small stones or gastroliths to grind the plant matter within the stomach.

The Sauropods of the Early Cretaceous

Throughout the Jurassic Period, many species became larger to outgrow the predators that hunted them. They became so large that an adult sauropod had no known enemies! No animal could withstand the force of a healthy sauropod weighing 80 to 100 tons, so size was a means of survival for the species. This was evident in the Early Cretaceous Period as well, with species like Argentinosaurus huinculensis and Sauroposeidon proteles, two of the largest sauropods to ever live. They were unimaginably large, yet they were born from eggs less than 8 inches in diameter (about the size of a volleyball).

A newborn was small enough to fit in one of your hands and later grew to be several thousand times its own size at maturity, unlike any animal on earth today. (Imagine an elephant hatching from a chicken's egg!)

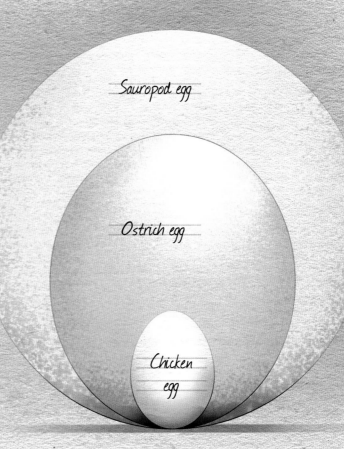

Sauropod egg

Ostrich egg

Chicken egg

Though their size was truly impressive, it was their distinct adaptations that made the sauropods so unique in the Early Cretaceous Period. Animals like the Nigersaurus taqueti developed an odd skull with a flat mouth, designed to eat parallel to the ground so it could maximize the amount of food with each bite. The front of its mouth was lined with 500 thin teeth, each sliding into the opposing tooth to act like a pair of shears, cutting ferns and cycads swiftly with each bite. The Amargasaurus cazaui was equally as strange; it developed a large crest with long spines protruding from its neck vertebrae to deter its predators and attract mates.

In the following pages we will take a look at how diversified the sauropods became in the Early Cretaceous Period. You'll get close enough to examine these extraordinary animals in fine detail, witnessing their impressive size and fascinating adaptations.

Amargasaurus cazaui

Location Observed: La Amarga, Argentina

Family: Dicraeosauridae

Length: 43 feet (15 meters)

Height: 8 feet (2.5 meters)

Weight: 6 tons

Temperament: Social, reclusive

Elongated spines along neck
with sharp spikes

Relatively short neck

Thick, sturdy legs

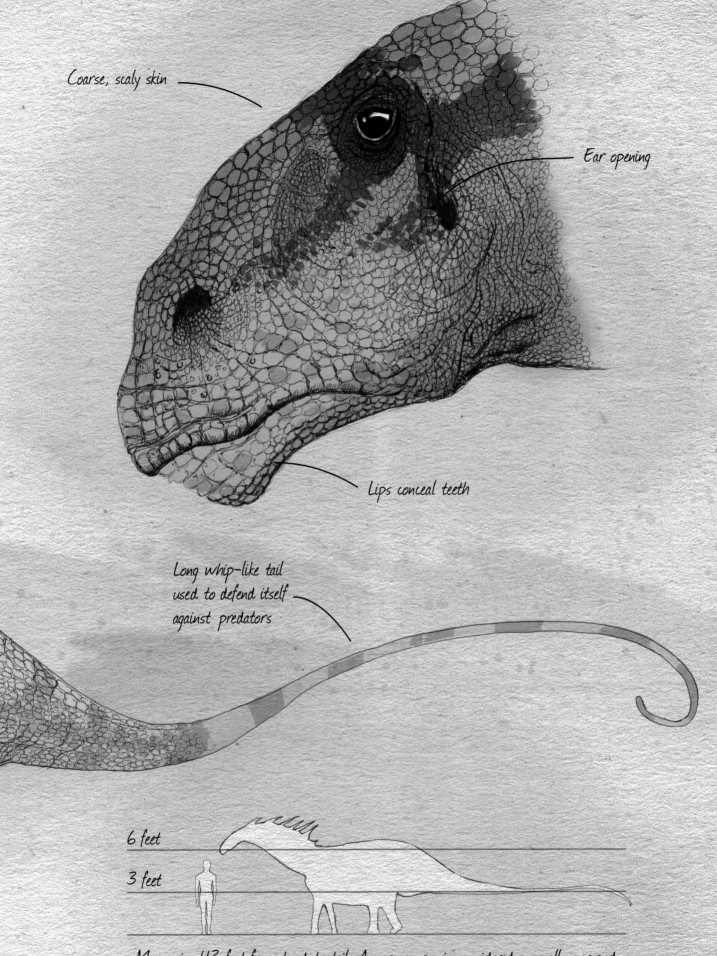

Coarse, scaly skin

Ear opening

Lips conceal teeth

Long whip-like tail
used to defend itself
against predators

6 feet

3 feet

Measuring 43 feet from head to tail, Amargasaurus is considered a small sauropod

59

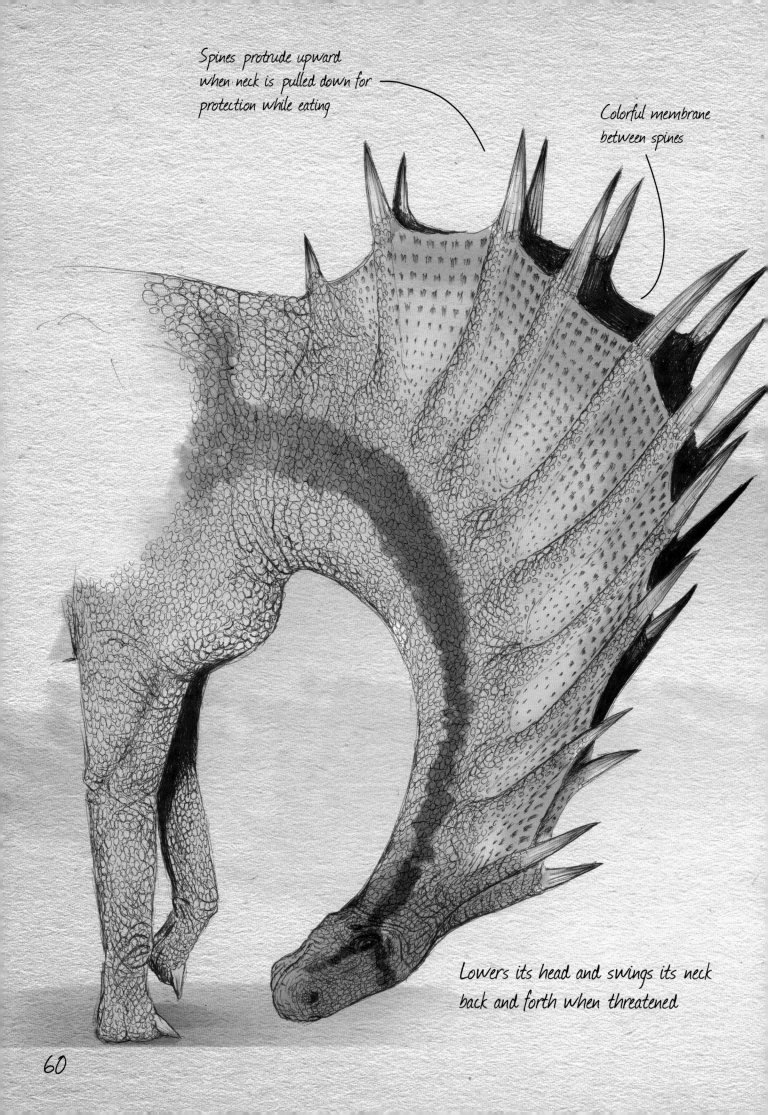

Spines protrude upward
when neck is pulled down for
protection while eating

Colorful membrane
between spines

Lowers its head and swings its neck
back and forth when threatened

60

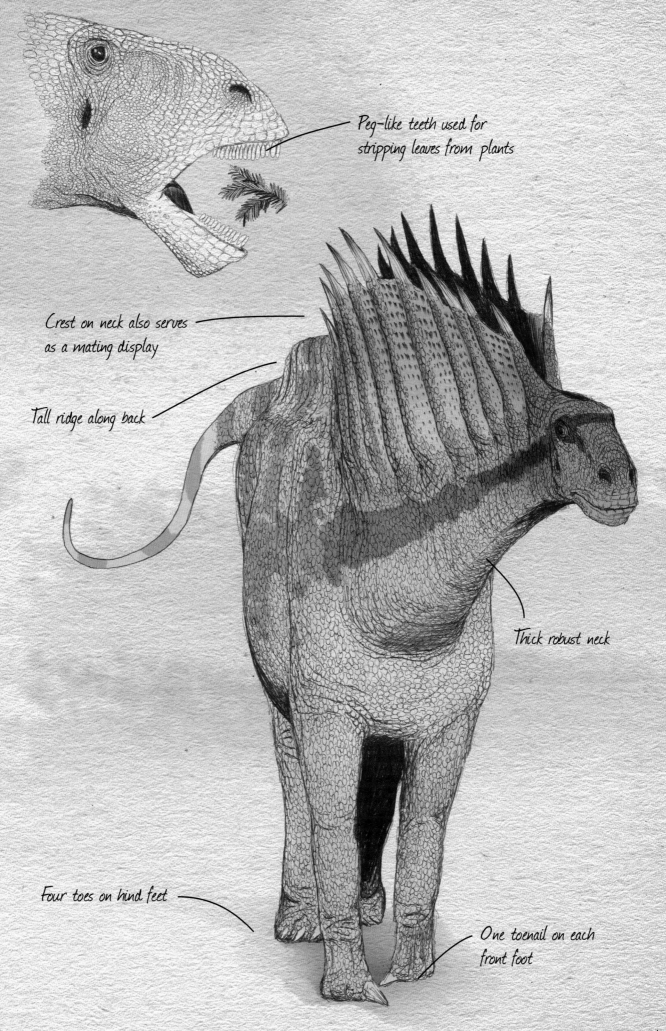

Peg-like teeth used for stripping leaves from plants

Crest on neck also serves as a mating display

Tall ridge along back

Thick robust neck

Four toes on hind feet

One toenail on each front foot

Argentinosaurus huinculensis

Long head

Location Observed: Huincul, Argentina

Family: Antarctosauridae

Length: 100 feet (30 meters)

Height: 60 feet (20 meters)

Weight: Over 50 tons

Temperament: Social, slow moving

Long, flexible neck

Longer forelimbs

Argentinosaurus is one of the largest animals to ever walk the earth

6 feet

3 feet

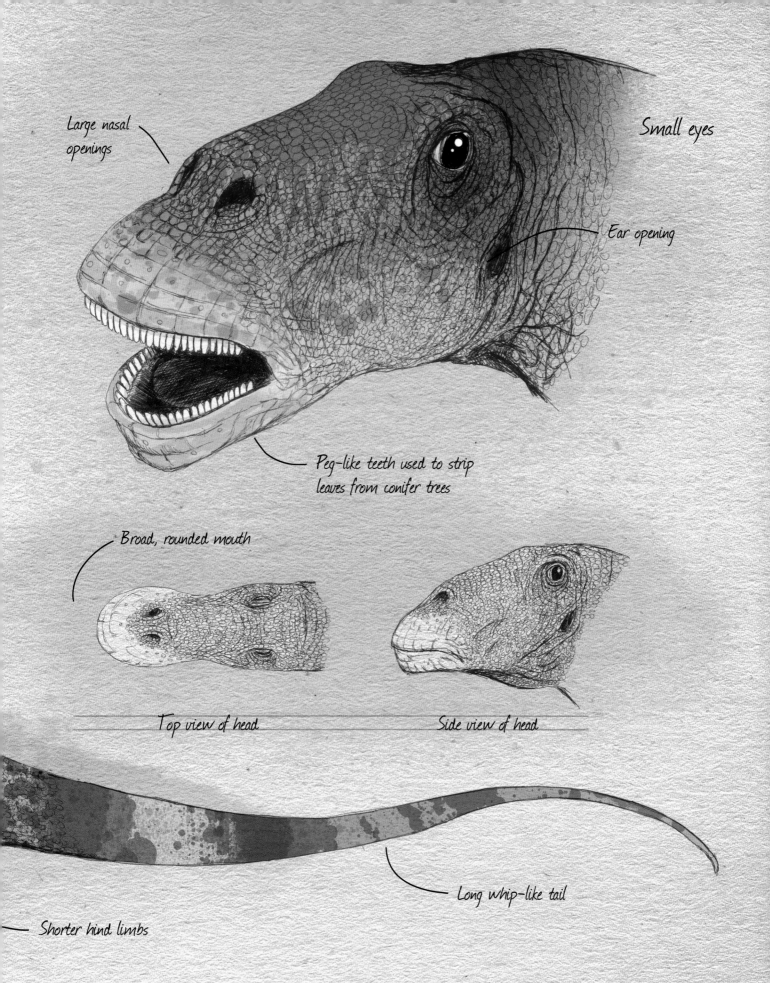

Large nasal openings

Small eyes

Ear opening

Peg-like teeth used to strip leaves from conifer trees

Broad, rounded mouth

Top view of head

Side view of head

Long whip-like tail

Shorter hind limbs

Neck capable of reaching both
tall trees and the ground to feed

Argentinosaurus primarily eats
the leaves and cones of conifer trees

A long, flexible tail whips in all
directions, making it impossible to
attack from behind

Three large, curved
toenails on rear feet

No toenails on front feet

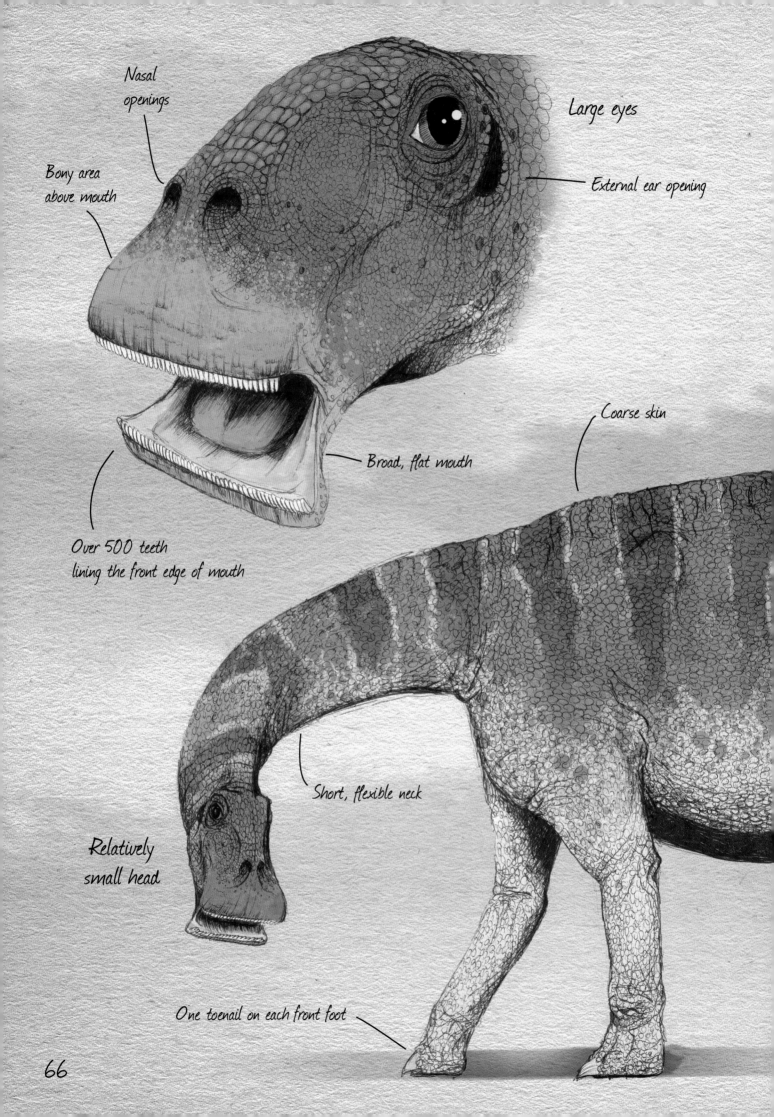

Nasal openings

Bony area above mouth

Large eyes

External ear opening

Broad, flat mouth

Over 500 teeth lining the front edge of mouth

Coarse skin

Short, flexible neck

Relatively small head

One toenail on each front foot

Nigersaurus taqueti

Location Observed: *Gadoufaoua, Republic of Niger*

Family: *Rebbachisauridae*

Length: *30 feet (9 meters)*

Height: *7 feet (2.2 meters)*

Weight: *2 tons*

Temperament: *Solitary, shy*

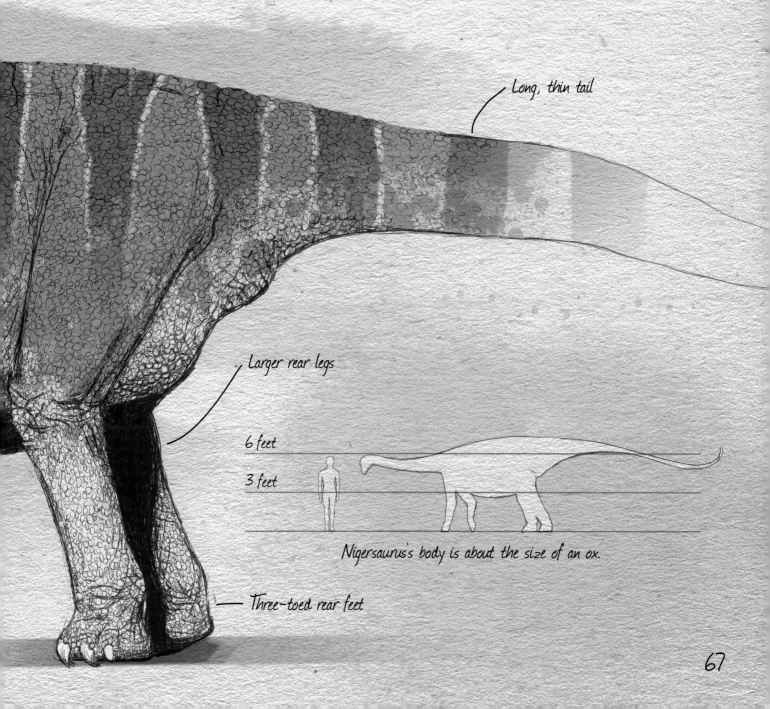

Long, thin tail

Larger rear legs

6 feet

3 feet

Nigersaurus's body is about the size of an ox.

Three-toed rear feet

Long, thin, whip-like tail acts as a defense to protect its hindquarters

Nigersaurus rears on its hind legs when threatened

Forelimbs used to defend itself

Lightly built skull positioned
facing downward

Bottom and top teeth
interlock to act like shears.
Worn teeth are constantly
replaced by new teeth.

Plants are sheared off
with each bite, leaving
only stumps

Nigersaurus eats mostly horsetail plants and ferns

Sauroposeidon proteles

Location Observed: Oklahoma, United States

Family: Brachiosauridae

Length: 90 feet (27 meters)

Height: 60 feet (18 meters)

Weight: 40 tons

Temperament: Social, territorial

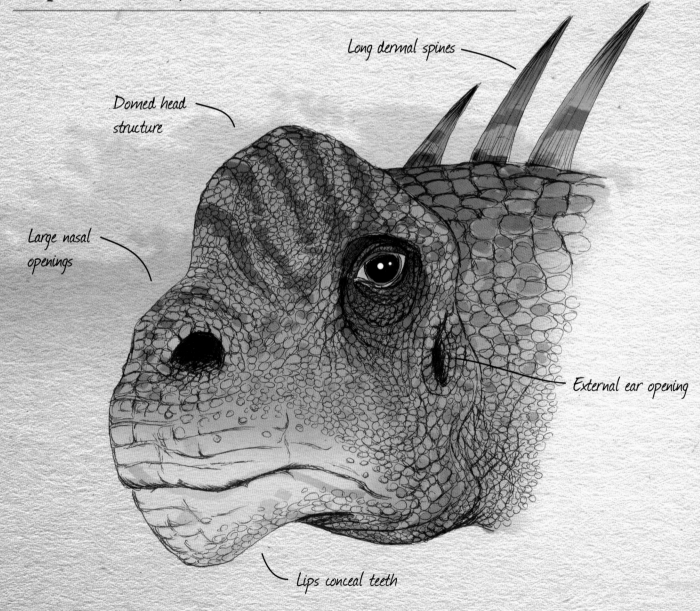

Long dermal spines

Domed head structure

Large nasal openings

External ear opening

Lips conceal teeth

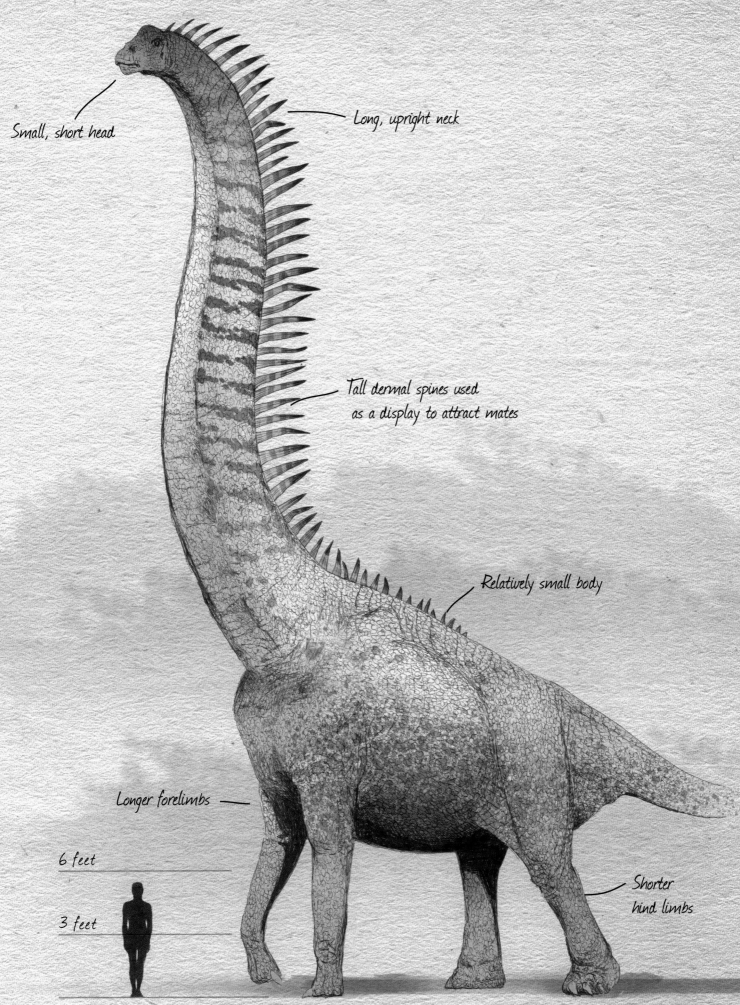

Small, short head

Long, upright neck

Tall dermal spines used
as a display to attract mates

Relatively small body

Longer forelimbs

6 feet

3 feet

Shorter
hind limbs

One of the tallest animals to ever walk the earth, Sauroposeidon towers over almost any animal

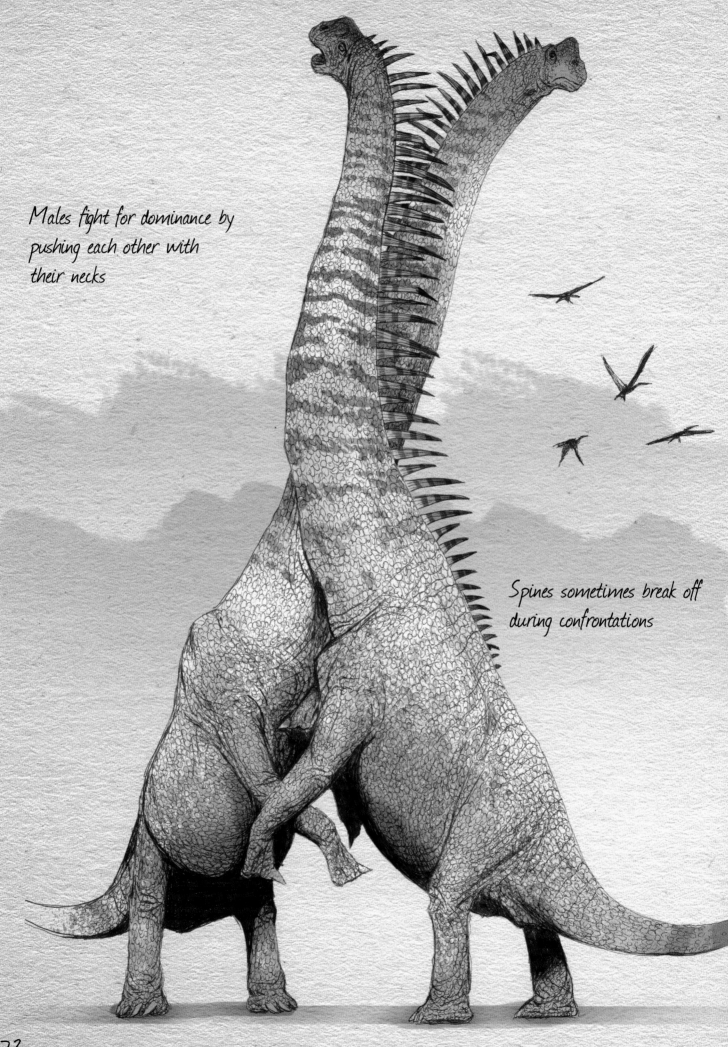

Males fight for dominance by pushing each other with their necks

Spines sometimes break off during confrontations

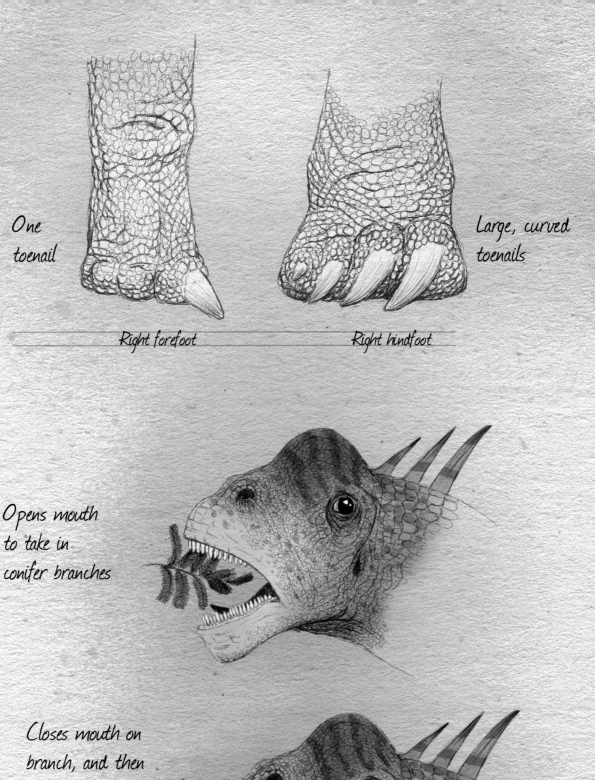

One
toenail

Large, curved
toenails

Right forefoot

Right hindfoot

Opens mouth
to take in
conifer branches

Closes mouth on
branch, and then
pulls back to
break from tree

Swallows whole
without chewing

Closes eye to prevent
injury from branches

Sauroposeidon feeding

The Ornithischians

You gaze across the Early Cretaceous landscape and see tall conifer trees in the distance with a field of fern and cycad plants before you. The weather is muggy and hot with sounds of insects and birds filling the air. The scenery is dotted with groups of large animals, about the size of elephants, slowly walking, then momentarily breaking stride to eat. Like modern-day antelope, they take turns raising their heads looking for potential danger. They continue on their way without much bother. Soon four armored animals join the group. They are lower to the ground but just as massive, all of them grazing on the plants beneath them. As one would come to expect, things don't remain calm for very long in the Cretaceous. All the animals become restless, some begin to make noise as they gather into a herd. A pack of six theropods have been hunting them. Now in the

6 feet

3 feet

open, they are in plain sight for the herd to see. The herd is tightly grouped and moving as if it were one animal. The theropods begin to charge in hopes of disbanding them, but they stay together leaving the theropods no option but to abandon the attack. Eventually, calm is restored as they all return to grazing. This is a typical day in the Early Cretaceous, and what it must have been like to be large prey, more specifically an ornithischian.

Ornithischians, meaning "bird-hipped," are an extremely diverse group of herbivorous dinosaurs characterized by their hip structure and beaks at the front of their jaws. They come in many forms—from large duck-billed animals resembling cattle to small parrot-like lizards to heavily armored walking fortresses. Because of this diversity, ornithischians are divided into three subgroups: thyreophorans, which include armored dinosaurs;

heterodontosaurs, which include the horned and frilled dinosaurs; and ornithopods, which include duck-billed dinosaurs.

The first ornithischians evolved in the Late Triassic and continued to thrive until the end of the Mesozoic, making them one of the most successful groups of plant-eating dinosaurs. All have hard beaks designed for snipping and cutting plants, while most have jaws lined with closely placed, leaf-shaped teeth used for grinding plant matter. Many in the species are exclusively quadrupeds. Some are capable of easily transitioning between moving on four legs and standing or running on two.

The Ornithischians of the Early Cretaceous

The Early Cretaceous is a transitory time for the ornithischians, seeing the emergence of species like Iguanodon bernissartensis, which are spreading across many continents. These are the great ancestors of what will soon be the hadrosaurs, or duck-billed dinosaurs. The Late Cretaceous sees the rise of the hadrosaur family as they flourish into an array of species, some with hollow crests and ornamental growths, and others that are larger and bulkier.

The Early Cretaceous is also a turning point for the ceratopsians. Species like Psittacosaurus mongoliensis, prolific in their numbers, are developing and are the ancestors to the great horned dinosaur: Triceratops.

This section delves into the diversity of ornithischians, with each of the three subgroups represented by key species that define the era.

Closely placed teeth for
grinding plant matter

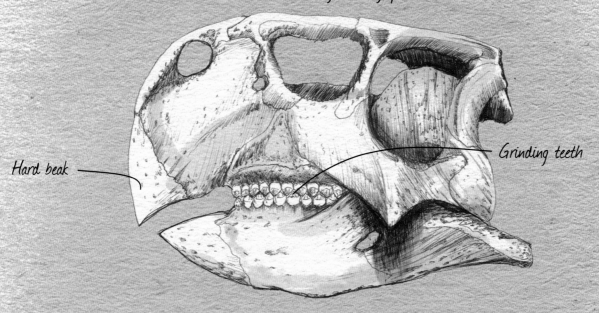

Hard beak

Grinding teeth

Psittacosaurus mongoliensis skull

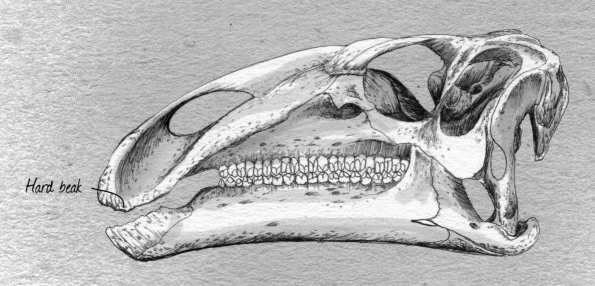

Hard beak

Iguanodon bernissartensis skull

Gastonia burgei

Location Observed: *Utah, United States*

Family: *Nodosauridae*

Length: *17 feet (5 meters)*

Height: *4 feet (1.3 meters)*

Weight: *1.9 tons*

Temperament: *Aggressive, solitary*

Thick, bony plates on back serve as armor

Wide, flat body

Short, sturdy legs

6 feet

3 feet

Gastonia weighs as much as a rhinoceros

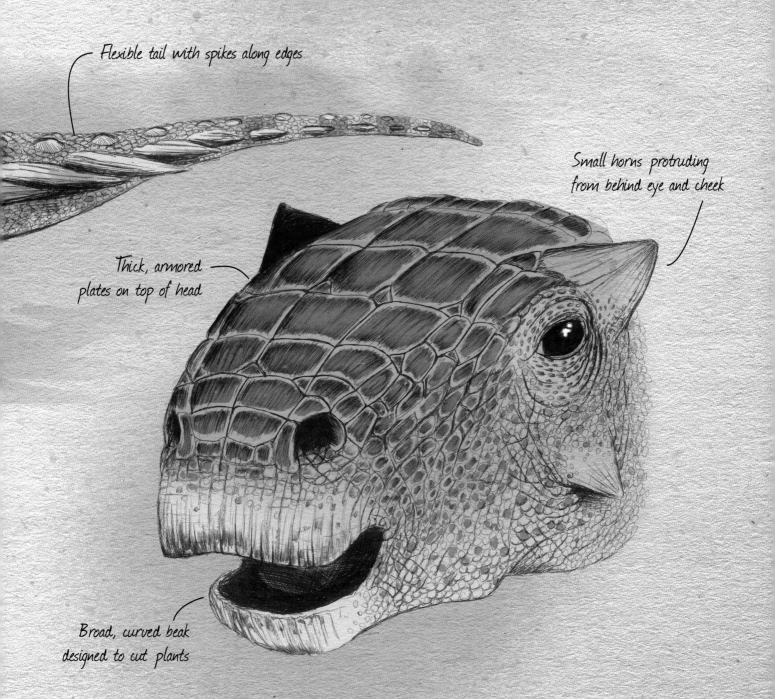

Flexible tail with spikes along edges

Small horns protruding from behind eye and cheek

Thick, armored plates on top of head

Broad, curved beak designed to cut plants

Gastonia's main defensive weapon is its tail

Very flexible and powerful, Gastonia's tail is used like an ax against attackers

When moved side to side, tail spikes fit into one another

Thick, bony plate provides protection from predators

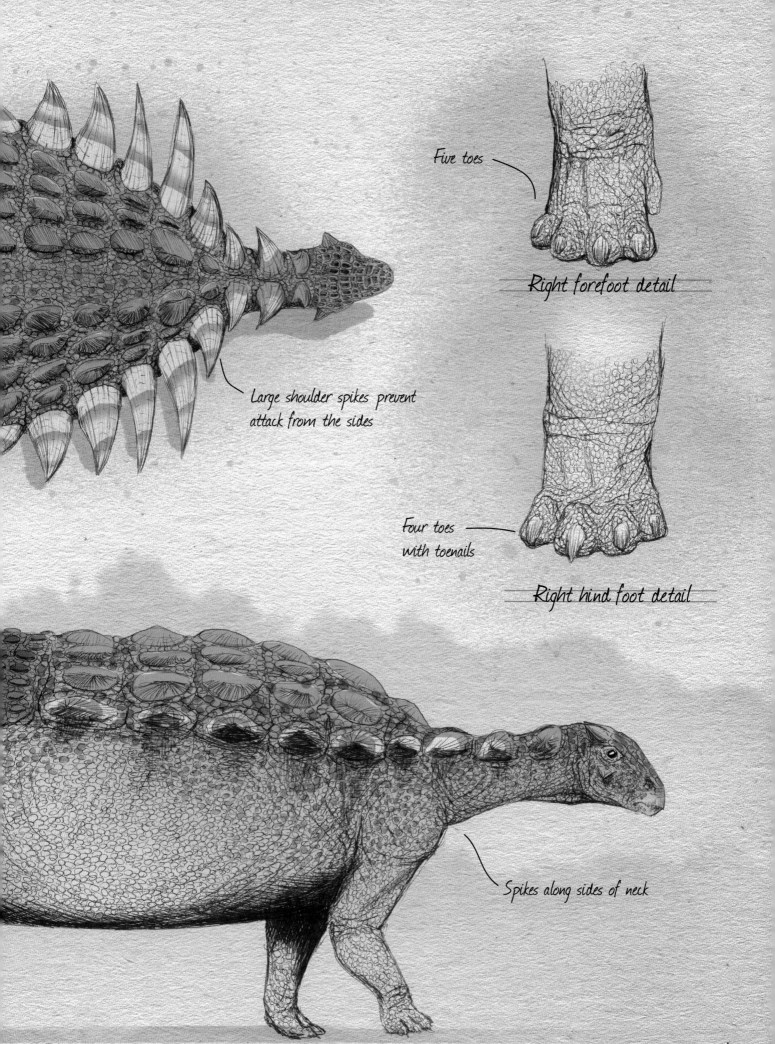

Five toes

Right forefoot detail

Large shoulder spikes prevent attack from the sides

Four toes with toenails

Right hind foot detail

Spikes along sides of neck

81

Iguanodon bernissartensis

Location Observed: *Utah, United States*

Family: *Iguanodontidae*

Length: *26 feet (8 meters)*

Height: *10 feet (3.1 meters)*

Weight: *3.2 tons*

Temperament: *Cautious, social*

Long, flexible neck

Thick, powerful legs

Larger hind limbs

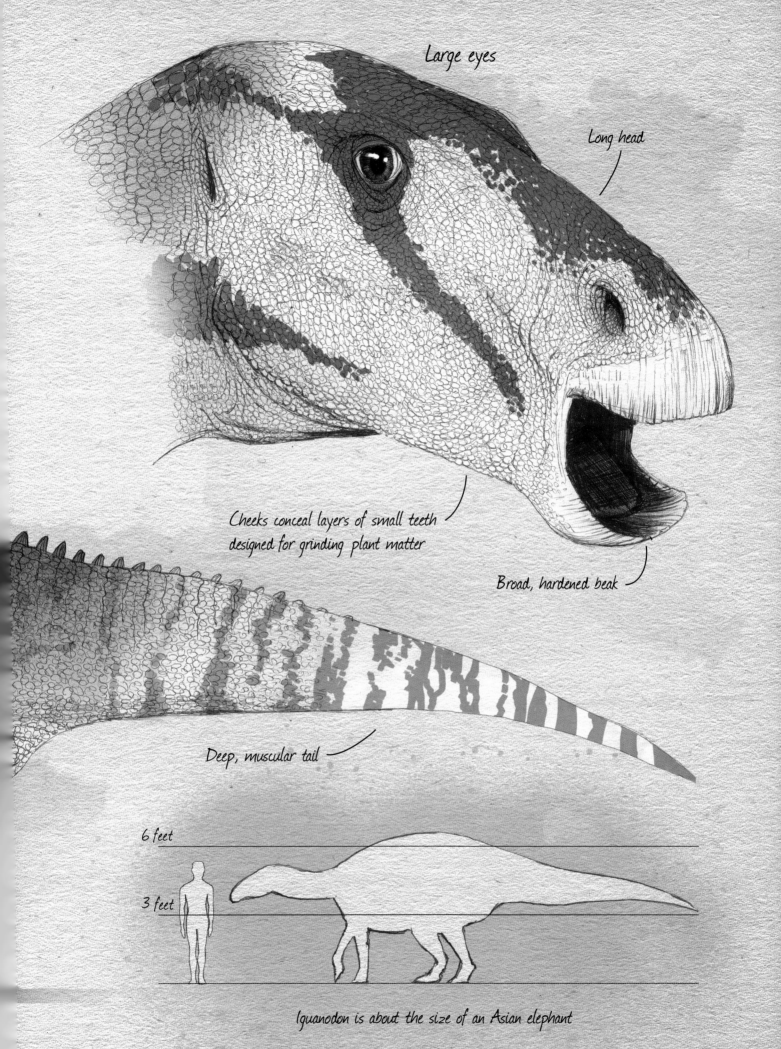

Large eyes

Long head

Cheeks conceal layers of small teeth
designed for grinding plant matter

Broad, hardened beak

Deep, muscular tail

6 feet

3 feet

Iguanodon is about the size of an Asian elephant

Primarily a quadruped walking
on all fours, but can walk and
run on two legs

Iguanodons live in large, familial herds
consisting of several generations

Iguanodons feed mostly on
low-growing plants

Broad, large hind feet
with long toes

Small, flexible toe
on outside of foot

Large "thumb" spike used
as a defensive weapon

Right foot detail

Right hand detail

Row of dermal spines
appear once mature

The young stay close to
the adults for protection

Ouranosaurus nigeriensis

Location Observed: *Niger, Africa*

Family: *Iguanodontidae*

Length: *27 feet (8.3 meters)*

Height: *10.5 feet (3.2 meters)*

Weight: *2.2 tons*

Temperament: *Social, cautious*

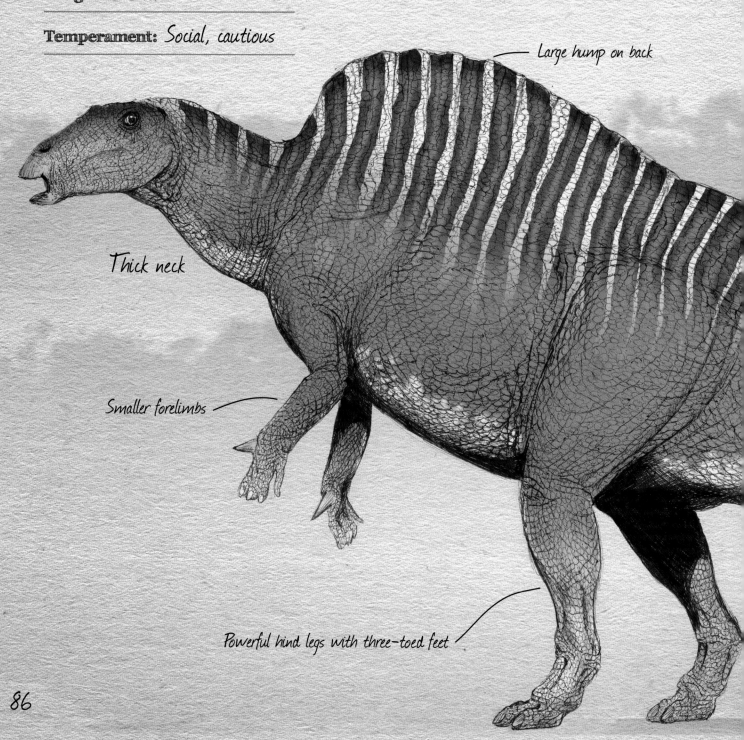

Large hump on back

Thick neck

Smaller forelimbs

Powerful hind legs with three-toed feet

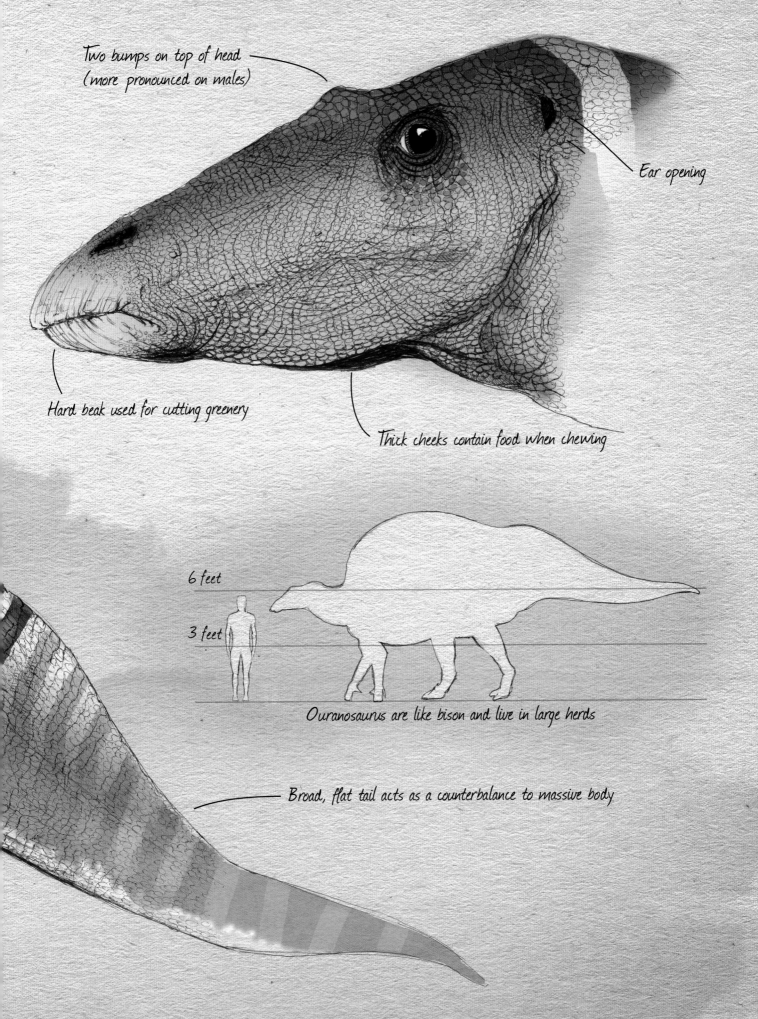

Two bumps on top of head
(more pronounced on males)

Ear opening

Hard beak used for cutting greenery

Thick cheeks contain food when chewing

6 feet

3 feet

Ouranosaurus are like bison and live in large herds

Broad, flat tail acts as a counterbalance to massive body

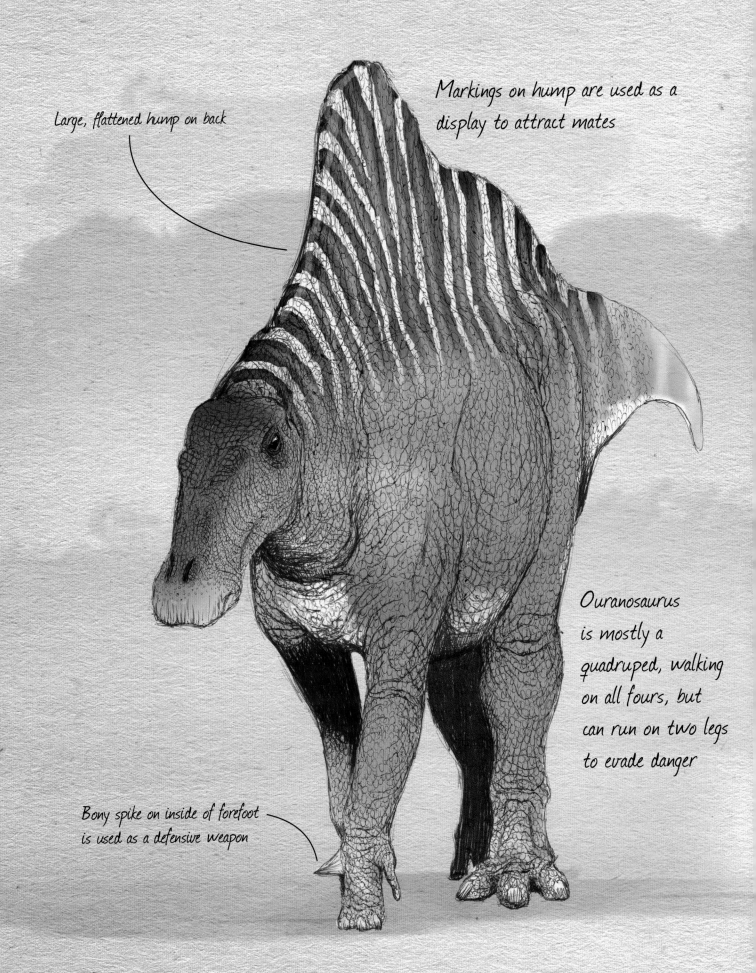

Large, flattened hump on back

Markings on hump are used as a display to attract mates

Ouranosaurus is mostly a quadruped, walking on all fours, but can run on two legs to evade danger

Bony spike on inside of forefoot is used as a defensive weapon

"Thumb" spike

Small, underdeveloped, flexible
toe on outside of foot

Foot pad

(Inside view of left hand)

Three main toes fused
together form the contact
point with the ground

Thick, fleshy foot splays to allow
secure footing on muddy ground

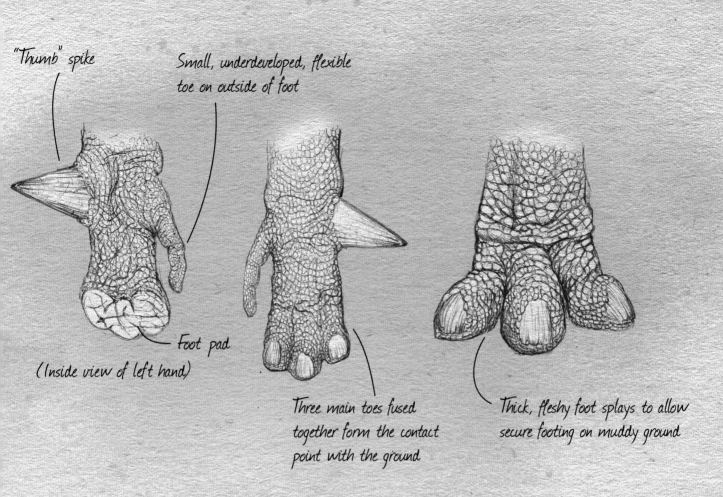

Left hand detail

Left foot detail

They live in large herds. The
young never leave the group.

2-year-old calf

Feeds mostly on ferns and cycads

Psittacosaurus mongoliensis

Location Observed: *Gobi Desert, Mongolia*

Family: *Ceratopsian*

Length: *5 feet (1.5 meters)*

Height: *2 feet (.8 meters)*

Weight: *35 lbs (15kg)*

Temperament: *Cautious, very social*

Long quills along back and tail used as a display to attract mates

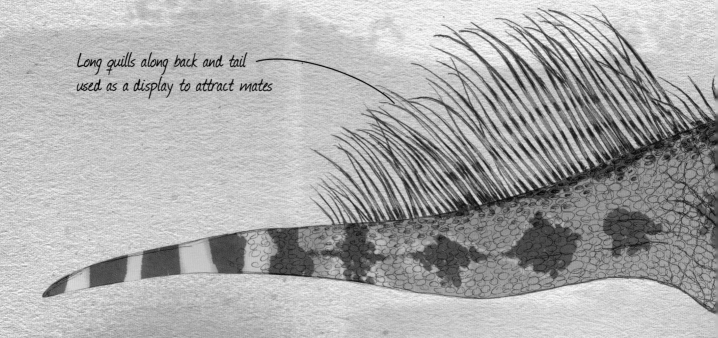

6 feet

3 feet

Strong hind limbs, capable of walking and standing on two legs

The adult Psittacosaurus is the size of a dog

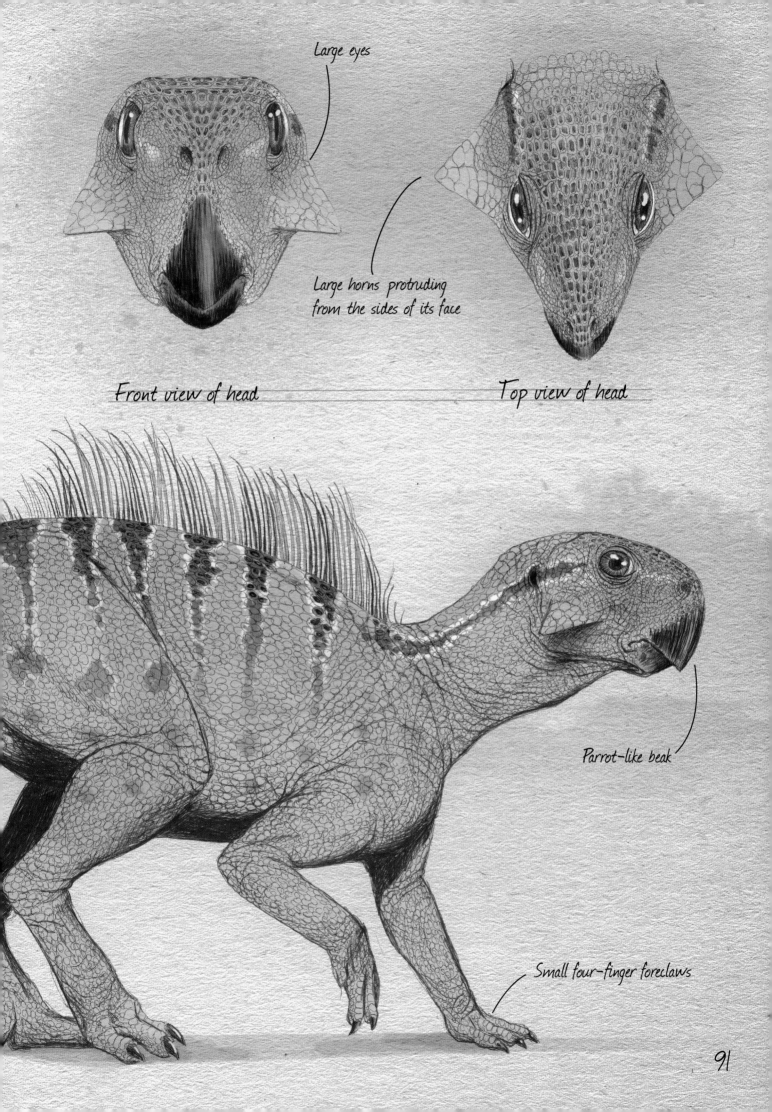

Large eyes

Large horns protruding
from the sides of its face

Front view of head　　　　　　　Top view of head

Parrot-like beak

Small four-finger foreclaws

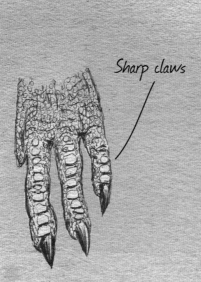

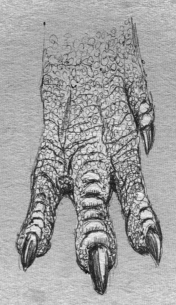

Sharp claws

Right foreclaw ————————————— Right hind foot

Psittacosaurus live in small family packs and spend
most of their time together foraging for food

Back quills are absent in females

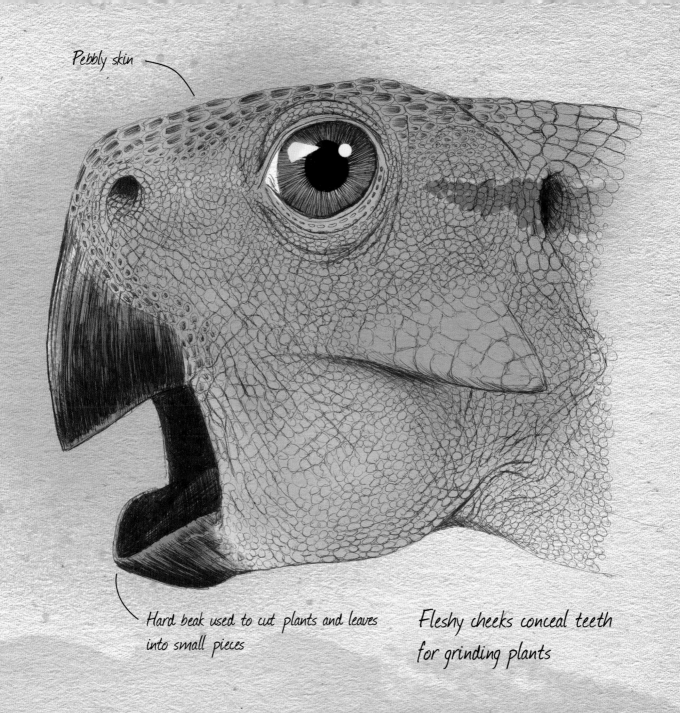

Pebbly skin

Hard beak used to cut plants and leaves into small pieces

Fleshy cheeks conceal teeth for grinding plants

At two months old, they are about the size of a rabbit and capable of evading predators

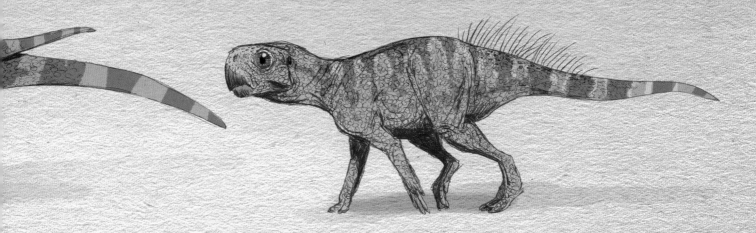

The Pterosaurs

As you walk through the sand and approach a river basin, you feel a large shadow drape over you. You look up and see an enormous flying creature gliding toward the shore. It pulls its wings up and, with a powerful thrust, forces them downward as it climbs higher. It scans the surface of the water below and locks its eyes on something. Slowly pulling its wings in, it dives toward the water with incredible speed. Within inches of reaching the surface, it spreads its massive wings and slows down. It then breaks the calm water with its long head and pulls out a fish in a single sweeping motion. The hunt doesn't go unnoticed. Two more arrive just as large as the first. They create a commotion, squawking and flapping as they try to take the prey from its toothy beak. The aerial battle continues as

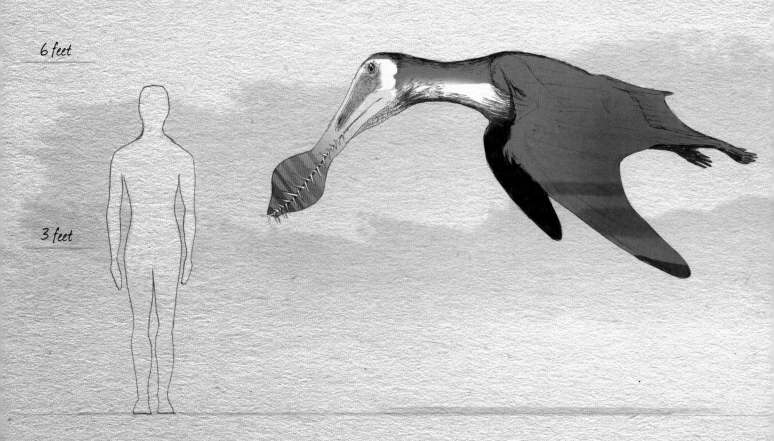

6 feet

3 feet

they fly higher. Finally, one grasps the head of the fish, tearing it away. The hunter, left with half a fish, flies off leaving the other two to battle over the stolen half. You just witnessed the pterosaurs of the Early Cretaceous—some of the largest animals ever to take flight.

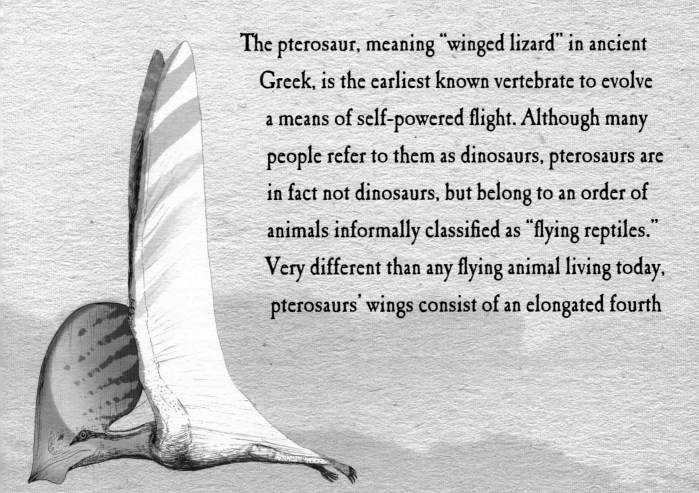

The pterosaur, meaning "winged lizard" in ancient Greek, is the earliest known vertebrate to evolve a means of self-powered flight. Although many people refer to them as dinosaurs, pterosaurs are in fact not dinosaurs, but belong to an order of animals informally classified as "flying reptiles." Very different than any flying animal living today, pterosaurs' wings consist of an elongated fourth finger with a fibrous membrane attaching the tip of the finger to the ankle of the hind leg. Their bodies are very small in comparison to their wings and head. All have air-filled, hollow bones with delicate skeletal structures. They are remarkably diverse in size; some have wingspans ranging from 10 inches, while others' reach over 30 feet—longer than a small aircraft.

Pterosaurs lived throughout most of the Mesozoic Era. The earliest species began to evolve in the Late Triassic period, with the latest going extinct at the end of the Cretaceous. The early pterosaurs had long tails and smaller heads and were smaller overall than later species. Pterosaurs' bodies were covered in a fine integument, or body covering, called "pycnofibres," which were similar to hair. Many, if not most, were piscatorial, meaning they hunted and fed on fish. Therefore some had developed long teeth designed to grasp and hold their prey. Others developed adaptations for feeding on small creatures along shorelines or hunting mid-air.

The Pterosaurs of the Early Cretaceous

By the Early Cretaceous period many species of pterosaurs had become significantly larger than their earlier ancestors. Their tails had reduced to a fraction of their original size, and their heads had become massive. Many had heads the size of their necks and torsos combined. Large crests began to evolve. These were used as displays to attract mates or to show dominance over rivals. By this period, pterosaur species had spread around the world, from Africa to Europe to South America.

The two species outlined in this book are Anhanguera blittersdorffi and Tapejara imperator; both are from South America and fed on fish. One is an example of a toothed pterosaur, while the other is an example of a toothless pterosaur. The following pages examine the animals that ruled the skies of the Early Cretaceous.

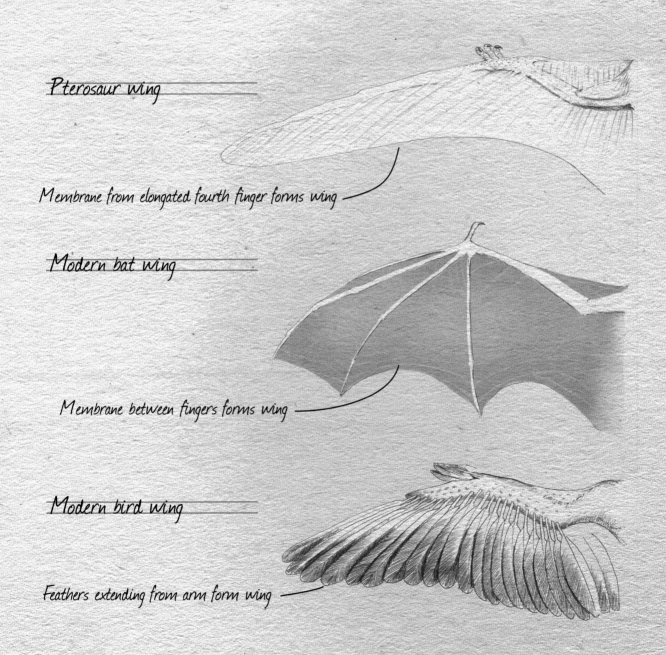

Pterosaur wing

Membrane from elongated fourth finger forms wing

Modern bat wing

Membrane between fingers forms wing

Modern bird wing

Feathers extending from arm form wing

Anhanguera blittersdorffi

Location Observed: *Brazil, South America*

Family: *Anhangueridae*

Length: *15 feet (4.5 meters) wingspan*

Height: *5 feet (1.5 meters) body length*

Weight: *33 lbs (15 kg)*

Temperament: *Aggressive*

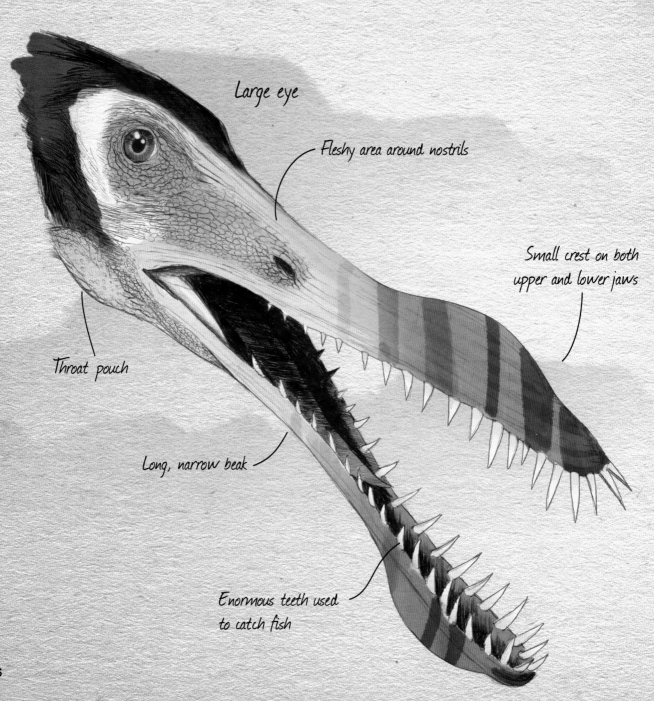

Large eye

Fleshy area around nostrils

Small crest on both upper and lower jaws

Throat pouch

Long, narrow beak

Enormous teeth used to catch fish

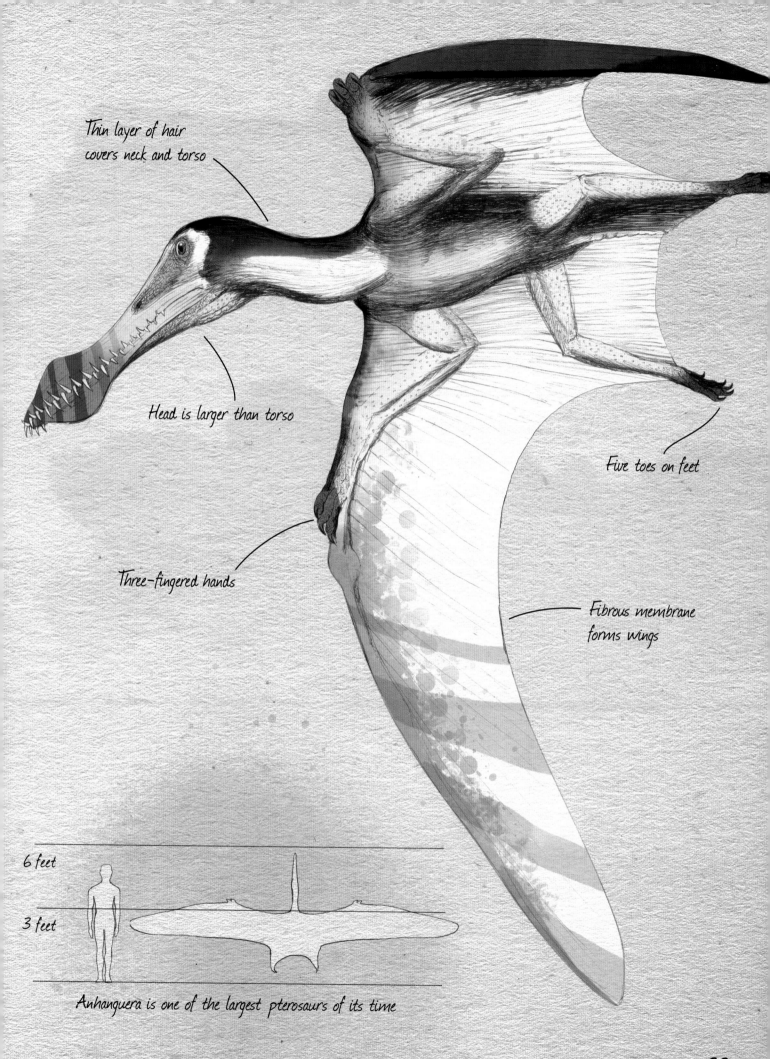

Thin layer of hair
covers neck and torso

Head is larger than torso

Three-fingered hands

Five toes on feet

Fibrous membrane
forms wings

6 feet

3 feet

Anhanguera is one of the largest pterosaurs of its time

Every meal was challenged.
Anhanguera was also an
opportunist, taking prey
from others in mid-flight.

Species of Fish Anhanguera Hunted

Vinctifer comptoni 3 feet (.9 meters)

Quadrupedal stance on ground

Sharp claws used
to secure footing

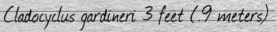
Cladocyclus gardineri 3 feet (.9 meters)

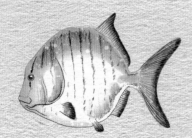

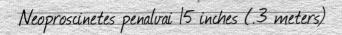
Neoproscinetes penalvai 15 inches (.3 meters)

Tharrhias araripis 16 inches (.4 meters)

Large crest on head

Small crest on chin

Three-fingered hands

Large crest on head

Tapejara imperator

Location Observed: Brazil, South America

Family: Tapejaridae

Length: 12 feet (3.6 meters) wingspan

Height: 3 feet (.6 meters) crest height

Weight: 26 lbs (12 kg)

Temperament: Social

Four-toed feet

Female

Male

Tapejara's crest is about half the size of its body length

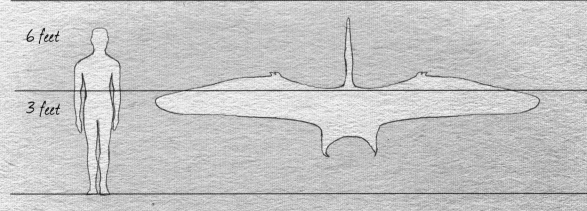

6 feet

3 feet

Eats while flying to protect its catch

Tapejara hunts primarily fish by skimming the surface of the water

Fourth finger forms the wing

Right hand detail

Right foot detail

Wings folded back

Tapejara walking on land

The First Birds

Imagine being a bird watcher in the Early Cretaceous. Looking up, you see the skies swarming with small birds. Along coastlines and waterways, you observe what look like flightless waterfowl floating on the surface, diving down momentarily, then popping back up with fish in their mouths. Overhead, flying alongside the pterosaurs, are birds much like modern seagulls or terns competing for fish. Considering the strange wildlife of the period, surprisingly, these birds look very similar to today's birds. Many act much like modern birds as well—jumping from branch to branch, chirping, eating seeds, and hunting small insects. These are early birds—not bird-like dinosaurs—with their own distinctive class. While the appearance may remind you of a finch or a crow, there are key differences. Most of these early birds have clawed hands on their wings and many still display teeth on their beaks, all vestiges of their ancestors, the theropod dinosaurs.

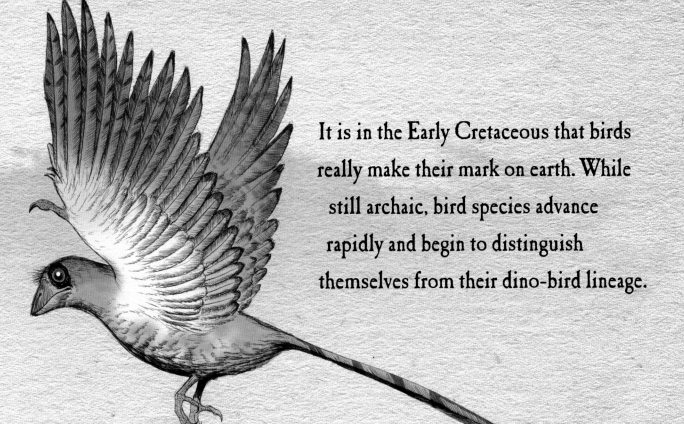

It is in the Early Cretaceous that birds really make their mark on earth. While still archaic, bird species advance rapidly and begin to distinguish themselves from their dino-bird lineage.

Their tails begin to disappear and wings become fuller and larger. Birds streamline the process of flying by developing feathers that contour to the shape of the body, making them more aerodynamic. Teeth get smaller and, in some species, disappear completely in favor of lighter beaks. The loss of their ancestors' long tails allows for dynamic flight and increased maneuverability in the air—an adaptation that is still visible in today's birds.

This section looks at two contrasting species: one an adept flier abundant in the Early Cretaceous skies; the other a toothed, flightless waterbird with adaptations for aquatic hunting. You'll notice the similarities right away, but look closely and you will see the remaining hints of their common ancestry with the dinosaurs.

Confuciusornis sanctus

Location Observed: Liaoning, China

Family: Confuciusornithidae

Length: 2.3 feet (.7 meters) wingspan

Height: 9 inches (22 centimeters) body length

Weight: .39 pounds (180 grams)

Temperament: Highly social

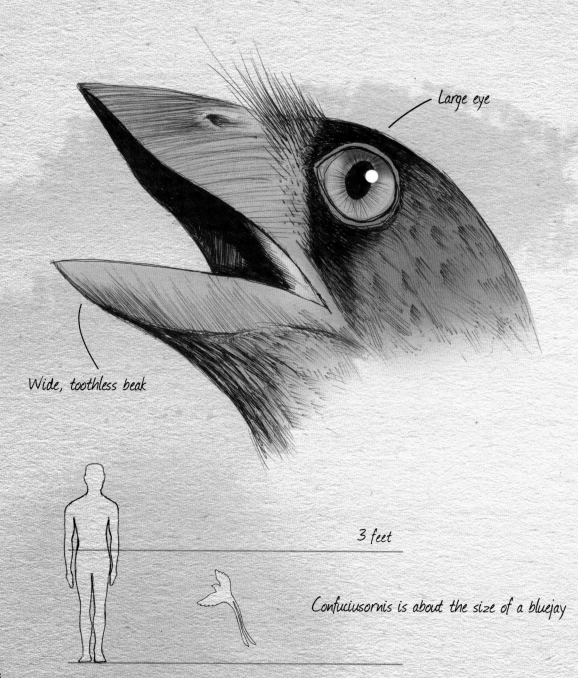

Large eye

Wide, toothless beak

3 feet

Confuciusornis is about the size of a bluejay

Two long feathers
to attract mates

Male Confuciusornis

Female Confuciusornis

Three claws on wing

Primary flight feathers
extremely long compared to
modern birds

Wing detail (underside)

109

Enaliornis barretti

Location Observed: London, England

Family: Enaliornithidae

Length: 1 foot (.3 meters) body

Height: 5 inches (12.7 centimeters) body width

Weight: 1 pound (.45 kilograms)

Temperament: Solitary, elusive

Long beak lined with small teeth used to catch fish

Small throat pouch

3 feet

Enaliornis is about the size of a large pigeon

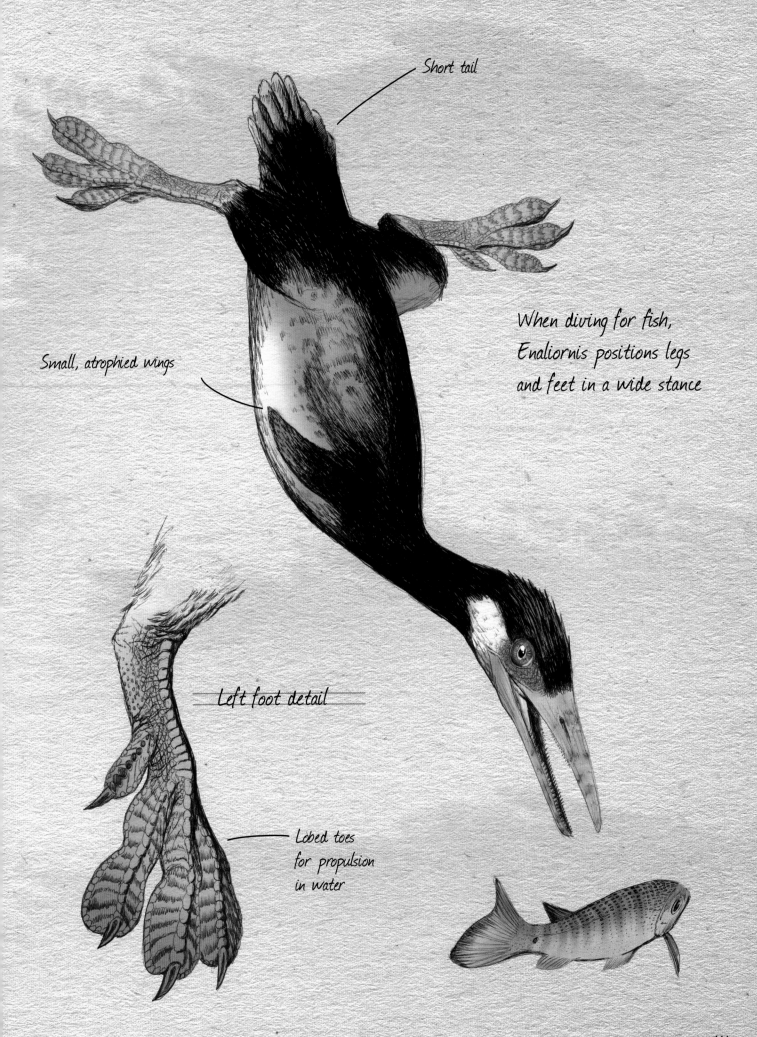

Short tail

Small, atrophied wings

When diving for fish,
Enaliornis positions legs
and feet in a wide stance

Left foot detail

Lobed toes
for propulsion
in water